This is a thoughtful, ambitious and encompassing exploration of what has made us modern. Going back to the 14th century and the collective trauma of the black plague as our starting point, Mukerji offers a counterpoint reading of modernity, emphasizing the role dreams, social forms and objects have had in conjuring humans anew. This is a tale told by a crafts-woman and a scholar full of nuance and detail, revealing in her attention to minutiae an immense topic. This book will force us to rethink what we know about modernity and culture.

Claudio E. Benzecry, Northwestern University,
author of *The Opera Fanatic*

Chandra Mukerji's take on modernity is wide-ranging, original, learned and alive with sights, sounds, and meaning. From fashion to philosophy to religious wars to the Parisian water supply, the book makes modernity poignantly real in its details and its broad sweep. A tour de force!

Robin Wagner-Pacifici, University in Exile Professor of Sociology,
New School for Social Research

Perhaps only Chandra Mukerji could write a book that glides so effortlessly across centuries, tackling selfhood and state-making, high fashion and digital games, imagination and despair. This reader-friendly volume is a stunning synthesis by a preeminent analyst of the cultures of modernity.

Steven Epstein, John C. Shaffer Professor,
Northwestern University

This is a remarkable book. Outstanding in its scope and ambition, outstanding too in the brevity and focus with which this ambition is realised. On the one hand it covers centuries of time, and does so with aplomb, guided by its main insight that cultural imaginaries and materiality have to be understood if modernity is to be understood. On the other hand, the narrative is constructed through the means of a myriad of brilliant cameos, ranging from its reconstruction of a world broken by the Black Death to contemporary film and video games. It is a very fine achievement.

Patrick Joyce, Emeritus Professor of History,
University of Manchester and Honorary Professor of History,
University of Edinburgh

MODERNITY REIMAGINED: AN ANALYTIC GUIDE

Winner of the American Sociological Association's *Distinguished Book Award* in 2012, Chandra Mukerji offers with this remarkable new book an explanation of the birth and subsequent proliferation of the many strands in the braid of modernity. The journey she takes us on is dedicated to teasing those strands apart, using forms of cultural analysis from the social sciences to approach history with fresh eyes. Faced with the problem of trying to understand what is hardest to see—the familiar—she gains analytic distance and clarity by juxtaposing cultural analysis with history, asking how modernity began and how people conjured into existence the world we now recognize as modern.

Part I describes the genesis of key modern social forms: the modern self, communities of strangers, the modern state, and the industrial world economy. Part II focuses on modern social types: races, genders, and childhood. Part III focuses on some of the cultural artifacts and activities of the contemporary world that people have invented and used to cope with the burdens of self-making, and to react against the broken promises of modern discourse and the silent injuries of material modernism.

Beautifully illustrated with over 100 color photographs in its ten chapters, *Modernity Reimagined* is not just an explanation, an analysis of how modern life came to be, it is also a *model* for how to *do* cultural thinking about today's world. The book's companion website at www.routledge.com/cw/mukerji provides a storehouse of additional images from the recent and not-so-recent past, as well as suggested exercises by the author so that readers can tease out their own additional strands from the braid of modern life.

Chandra Mukerji is known among students and scholars of culture as one of the titans of the field, primarily because she crosses intellectual and disciplinary boundaries with ease, and also because she has written so many prize-winning books that have astonished colleagues for their range and original insight. She has won the American Sociological Association's distinguished book award, the Merton Award from the SKAT section of the ASA, and the Douglas prize from the Culture section, all for different publications, but each examining important historical examples of how materiality shapes social life. In tandem with her scholarly publications, she also taught a broad array of courses at the University of California, San Diego to undergraduates—where she encouraged students to "theorize about culture"—examining material, social, and organizational forms in original ways.

ALSO BY CHANDRA MUKERJI:

From Graven Images: Patterns of Modern Materialism (New York: Columbia University Press, 1983).

A Fragile Power (Princeton: Princeton University Press, 1990).

Rethinking Popular Culture, co-edited with Michael Schudson (University of California Press, 1990).

Territorial Ambitions and the Gardens of Versailles (Cambridge University Press, 1997).

Impossible Engineering: Technology and Territoriality on the Canal du Midi (Princeton University Press, 2009).

Upcoming Related Routledge Titles:

Is Paris Still the Capital of the Nineteenth Century?: Essays on Art and Modernity, 1850–1900, edited by Hollis Clayson and Andre Dombrowski.

Imaginaries of Modernity: Politics, Cultures, Tensions, by John Rundell.

Early Modern Emotions: An Introduction, edited by Susan Broomhall.

Authority and Spectacle in Medieval and Early Modern Europe: Essays in Honor of Teofilo Ruiz, by Yuen-Gen Liang and Jarbel Rodriguez.

Constructing the Viennese Modern Body: Art, Hysteria and the Puppet, by Nathan J. Timpano.

Modernity Reimagined: An Analytic Guide

Chandra Mukerji

Routledge
Taylor & Francis Group

NEW YORK AND LONDON

First published 2017
by Routledge
711 Third Avenue, New York, NY 10017

and by Routledge
2 Park Square, Milton Park, Abingdon, Oxon, OX14 4RN

Routledge is an imprint of the Taylor & Francis Group, an informa business
© 2017 Taylor & Francis

Library of Congress Cataloging in Publication Data
A catalog record for this book has been requested

ISBN: 978-1-138-82533-8 (hbk)
ISBN: 978-1-138-82534-5 (pbk)
ISBN: 978-1-315-74005-8 (ebk)

Typeset in Adobe Caslon Pro
by Cenveo Publisher Services

The author has developed an archive of historical materials and a set of pedagogical exercises based on them that instructors can use (or not), and these are located on the publisher's website associated with this book. The website can be found at **www.routledge.com/cw/mukerji**. Additional information about the archive and exercises can be found in the Appendix on Teaching Resources at the back of this book.

Printed and bound in the United States of America by Sheridan

In memory of my grandparents who taught me to think about history, and who demonstrated to me the grief of modernity with their words, lives, and deaths: Robert Childers Barton, Ethyl Dugan Mukerji, and Dhan Gopal Mukerji

Contents in Brief

Part One
History of Modern Social Forms

Part Two
Genealogies of Modern Social Types

Contents in Detail

Part Three
Popular Tools of Modern Life

LIST OF FIGURES

LIST OF TABLES

PREFACE
ORIGINS AND THE ANALYSIS OF MODERNITY

Modernity is a culture of survival and reinvention that has altered the relationship between people and the environment, using dreams of possibility and material means to address experiences of dislocation and discontent. It has spread historically with destructive force, as people take down old worlds to build new ones. It is as economically and politically expansive as it is destructive, so modernity seems to hold out hope of change for the better. But the modern world is also plagued by wars between competing states, and it is powered by fossil fuels that are being depleted, destroying the environment as they go. As a result, modernity, while offering opportunities, also poses problems of huge proportions.

Unfortunately, we know relatively little about it. We attribute its mixture of destruction and creation to capitalism, not to culture. We locate the genesis of modern culture in the 18th and 19th centuries when Enlightenment philosophers articulated principles of progress that were used to spur the development of global industrial capitalism. But modernity existed well before the 18th century, and understanding its early forms provides keys to understanding its contemporary unfolding.

We mistakenly assume modernity to be tolerant and moderate when historically it has been the opposite, drawing lines of invidious distinction among religions, races, genders, age grades, sexualities, and classes. We treat modern alienation and anomie as products of economic forces, completely ignoring the terrible grief caused by the physical destruction of worlds and communities in pursuit of modern progress. We treat materialism as a quasi-psychological problem, commodity fetishism, rather than a radical turn to things as impersonal mediators and sources of comfort in modern worlds of strangers. We often treat modernity as a period in human history, too, rather than a culture, ignoring the power of the cultural imaginaries that drive it, the improvised nature of modern life, the anxieties that run through it, the loneliness in communities of strangers, the material conceptions of progress, and the difficulty of learning to live in a culture that has divisive standards, but whose hierarchies are naturalized. Bruno Latour says we have never been modern, comparing Europeans to Africans as exemplary non-moderns.[1] But I say we have *all* been modern for centuries—just in different ways—because no part of the world has been untouched by modernity.[2] Slaves became just as modern as their masters in serving the construction of plantation agriculture. There are many strands in the braid of modernity, and this book is dedicated to teasing them apart, using forms of cultural analysis from the social sciences to approach history with fresh eyes.

To do this kind of cultural analysis, I rely on analytic traditions from the modern world itself.[3] So, I am faced with the problem of trying to understand what is hardest to see: the familiar. I gain my analytic distance—such as it is—by juxtaposing cultural analysis to history, asking how modernity began and how people conjured into existence the world we now recognize as modern. Modernity is the culture of the new, but I ask what has modernity been in the past? The answer I give is alternately familiar and not. I locate modernity much earlier than most cultural analysts—in the 14th century with the Black Death, when so many people died that survivors found it hard to live as they had before. Whole trades were lost in towns where no one remained with the skills to do the work. Whole families vanished, too, and in many areas, there were too few people remaining to till the fields or bring in the harvest. Survivors were richer because property was shared among fewer people, but no one could feel they really deserved it. It was an anomic situation, confusing because personal standing changed so fast. Survivors had to act differently, and when they did, they violated codes of conduct that no longer made sense to them. They picked up shards of the world they knew, and used them to fashion a world they had to dream up and try to make real.

Taking the plague as the starting point for modernity is familiar, if not unchallenged, as a form of periodization among historians, but tracing modernity as a culture back this far is something that cultural analysts rarely do. Modernity seen from this perspective is different—from its inception an expression of human creativity and will in the face of despair, and a radical reordering of people and things. A microbe tore European society apart, and God did not save the faithful any more than the sinners. For Catholic Europe, it left an unspeakable void in families, communities, and faith that survivors had to fill.

This specter of nature striking people with a devastating blow that more than halved communities, families, and the labor force provides a different perspective on the genesis of modernity than heroic tales of European Enlightenment or industrial innovation. Neither does it fit stories of the dehumanizing alienation engendered by capitalism or the anxieties caused by modern discourse. It describes a modernity born in grief and anomie in which survivors of traumatic loss started improvising what to do next. The first

[1] Burno Latour, *We Have Never Been Modern* (Cambridge: Harvard University Press, 1993).
[2] Anna Tsing, *The Mushroom at the End of the World* (Princeton: Princeton University Press, 2015).
[3] Zine Magubane, "American Sociology's Racial Ontology: Remembering Slavery, Deconstructing Modernity, and Charting the Future of Global Historical Sociology," *Cultural Sociology*, online, May 6, 2016.

moderns stepped into the unknown of their own lives with uncertainty, the same kind of uncertainty immigrants, refugees, the alienated, poor people, and the young carry into modern life today.

By my account, modernity was born of an environmental crisis that wiped out rats and other animals as well as people. Fields left untended started to turn back to forests as trees claimed them. Towns that were abandoned by people were adopted by other animals. This is the modernity we need to understand better to consider climate change seriously. It shows what natural catastrophe means, and how radically lives can be altered in short order. It also provides a way to understand how moderns became so attached to manufactured goods that they threatened the planet to make lots of them. With so many familiar faces gone, the survivors of the Black Death started taking new interest in things, simultaneously covering themselves with signs of piety and stimulating capitalist trade by doing it with luxurious textiles. The elites who could afford it became self-fashioning individuals, using clothing to address their guilt and grief and to build new identities. They used hats and bodices, furs and jewelry to express their aspirations, hoping that what had been lost could be replaced by something better. So, modern material desires grew out of heartbreak—the need to leave others behind and proceed, relying on only remnants of the past.

Looking at the modern world in this early form allows us to appreciate the improvisation endemic to modernity. Like jazz, it is a way of exploring possibilities with others, using cultural instruments and precedents to make something new. There is difficulty finding common direction. Not everyone wants to create the same future or live the same way, raising questions about how to deal with difference.

We usually assume religious tolerance to be distinctly modern, but intolerance was endemic to the Reformation and the Wars of Religion in the 16th into the 17th century. Members of the Reformed faiths, as modern selves reinventing Christianity, wanted to make religion less corrupt, taking personal responsibility for their moral standing and seeking personal knowledge of God through reading the Bible. Their impulses were modern, but just as destructive as they were visionary. Reformers wanted to take down the old church to create a new one, treating Catholicism and Catholics as degraded and immoral —legitimate objects of violence and hatred. The Catholic Church, in turn, sought to stamp out opposition by force, as it had done for centuries, destroying heresies to maintain its power. The result was raging hatred, virulent intolerance, and warring factions of Christian soldiers fighting for God. The use of propaganda to inflame the passions helped spread war across Europe, and forced even more people to become displaced from their homes and to seek new ways of life. This was the modernity of violence and intolerance that Europe nurtured, and exported to distant places to establish colonies.

What made early modernity distinctive was not secularism and rationality but rather destruction and dreams of possibility. Self-fashioning individuals now found themselves living in history as the world changed around them, and taking responsibility for the future. Imperial ambitions became potent, too, fed by stories of ancient empires—both fictional and fact—that suggested what else there was to do. Merchants in trading companies dreamt of finding the land of Prester John, building fortunes and commercial empires by trading around the world. Political leaders, faced with stories of the glory of Rome, nurtured dreams of imperial destiny that were used to empower modern states. Modern imaginaries were partly material, too, dreams of dominion over the earth and its creatures—Christian stewardship transformed into property relations. These dreams justified exploitation of nature to serve human purposes. And dreams of classical revival also stimulated material experiments in art, performance, engineering, and trade.

It is only against this background of cultural imagining and improvisation of early modernity that we can appreciate how profoundly the articulation of the characteristics and measures of modernity changed in the "long" 18th century (late 17th to 18th). There is a reason that cultural critics trace modernity back to this period of the Enlightenment when ideas of progress defined modernity as the highest level of human achievement. Modern discourse, once shared, became common sense, and provided the logic of legitimate action. The principles served as standards against which people and their lives were measured. It was the responsibility of all modern selves to "invest" in themselves and their futures. Speculating on economic futures even became standard practice in the 19th century as capitalists placed bets on the future value of commodities. Modernity defined forms of rationality, not the other way around.

This book tells a story of modernity rooted in grief, dreams, and discourse, and follows these cultural elements into the contemporary world. It is a tale of survival, destruction, and reinvention only possible to see through different forms of cultural analysis. So, this book has three parts.

Part I describes the genesis of key modern social forms: the modern self, communities of strangers, the modern state, and the industrial world economy. It looks at the growth of modernity before it was articulated, and illustrates how it changed in the Enlightenment and with industrial capitalism. The chapters emphasize the importance of cultural imaginaries to the development of modernity, tracing how modern selves, communities, and states were conjured up and made real. It also shows what happened to modern selves, lives, cities, and nations when modernity was articulated and its principles internalized as common sense. Each chapter focuses on one form—one social strand in the braid of modern culture. The chapters do not describe a single chronology for all modernity because this culture did not develop as a whole, but piecemeal, new strands of modern life braiding into what existed already. Still, the chapters introduce early modern social forms roughly in sequence.

Part II focuses on modern social types: races, genders, and age grades. It looks more deeply into how important the power of discourse—particularly scientific discourse—was in forming modern social relations of power. Efforts to identify natural distinctions ran up against the geopolitical and economic reasons to do so, yielding race and gender categories that were too inconsistent and obviously biased to naturalize effectively. Child development, on the other hand, succeeded in describing children as natural kinds. The politics were less obvious because they were not intended to distinguish among children, but rather define children as a whole. But the image of natural development in children was even more essential to modern discourses of power. In developmental theories, children recapitulated in their lives the progress of human civilization from primitive (baby) to modern (adult). So, child development reinforced the dominant image of human progress, equating full adulthood with Western education.

Part III focuses on some of the cultural artifacts and activities of the contemporary world that people have invented and used to cope with the burdens of self-making and to react against the broken promises of modern discourse and the silent injuries of material modernism. There are many examples that could be explored, but I have chosen three: digital maze games, films about humanity and inhumanity, and what I call escape routes, efforts to reach beyond the constraints of modernity through art and politics.

I chose the digital games because they are technological elements of modern culture that employ an ancient form: the maze. So, they address both problems endemic to human life and particular problems of modernity. I chose films because they provide points of reflexivity about human conduct and character. The contrast between human stories and the inhuman machinery of the medium poses questions about what it means to be human or be a machine. And I look at movements in art and for social justice to see how people invent means to escape or counter the injuries of modern life. These forms are themselves deeply modern, part of the restlessness of selves charged with responsibility for reinventing themselves and the future. They take modernity in new directions, recapturing the power of dreaming in modern life that has been generally eclipsed by discourse.

Chandra Mukerji
Del Mar, CA

The author has developed an archive of historical materials and set of pedagogical exercises based on them that instructors can use (or not), and these are located on the publisher's website associated with this book. The website can be found at **www. routledge.com/cw/mukerji**. Additional information about the archive and exercises can be found in the Appendix on Teaching Resources at the back of this book.

ACKNOWLEDGMENTS

I would like to thank Steve Rutter at Taylor and Francis for his guidance of this project through changes of editors at the publishing house, and the ups and downs in my own life. I have needed his companionship on this journey, and I am grateful to Doug Hartmann for suggesting we meet. I am also happy Taylor and Francis wanted me to develop an online archive to use in teaching with this book. I think it is important for students to look for patterns in primary material and think about problems of interpretation and history. It is hard to organize these opportunities for classes when you have many different ones to teach, so I am happy to help tired teachers with resources for their classes. The pedagogical principle of having students work with archival material is sound, and I am grateful that Steve Rutter has helped me acquire material for the website. I am grateful for the careful editorial readings of the manuscript by Athena Bryan and Sarah Cheeseman that prevented me from embarrassing myself too much.

I want to thank a number of colleagues who talked to me about this project or parts of it. Most notably, I need to thank Lilly Irani who has read more than a few drafts of chapters, and given me wonderful comments on them. I also want to thank other wonderful and groundbreaking San Diego colleagues who have helped me think about materiality and culture, including Fernando Dominguez-Rubio, Mary Walshok, and Kelly Gates. I am also grateful to Marion Fourcade, Claudio Benzrecy, and Geneviève Zubrzycki for keeping my interest alive in cultural analysis at the intersection of history and sociology. The chance to talk with them about issues of culture has been a pleasure and an inspiration.

I owe the most thanks to the graduate students who have helped me with this project, mostly members of my graduate writing group. Monica Hoffman not only read chapters and made editorial suggestions, but also helped find images for the book and the archive. Katie Simpson did editorial work, too, and engaged me in interesting discussions about the project as she was making corrections on drafts. Reece Peck and John Armenta may not remember this, but both urged me to work on the film analysis that ended up in Chapter 9. They saw early efforts on my part to describe film as philosophical machinery, and made me promise not to drop this line of inquiry even after a few film analysts found what I was doing inadequate. Marisa Brandt, Kim De Wolff, and Stephen Mandiberg all gave me good guidance in thinking about digital games and modernity, and Jonathan Walton introduced me to Monument Valley—one of my favorite games. Kara Wentworth not only talked to me about many of my ideas, but also linked what I was doing to work she liked in Anthropology, making the analysis more sophisticated than it would have been without her. And Sarah Klein and Anna Starshinina helped me with the proposal for this book, and maintained an interest in the emerging manuscript that warmed my heart when the work was hard.

Many other colleagues outside the US have been influential, too, particularly Kapil Raj who spent hours in Paris talking with me about modernity, what it was, and problems of periodization. Patrick Joyce helped me understand better connections between materiality and aspects of industrial and discursive modernity with his work on materiality and little tools of knowledge. And Claude Rosental helped me think about inarticulacy through his work on demonstrations, looking at the absurdity and efficacy of acts whose significance was hard to define.

I am grateful, too, to many historians of science who helped me think about modernity and materiality, such as Paola Bertucci, Harold Cook, Pamela Smith, Kapil Raj, and Karl Appuhn. They have made me understand better the circulation of ideas, people, and things, and what it has meant historically to inhabit trading zones, territories, and traditions of skill.

I have presented early versions of some parts of chapters at a number of conferences where I received generous feedback. The Consuming Passions Conference at Washington University gave me a chance to think out loud about Colbert's art program and the French state. I learned to see French history differently from the responses of Harriet Stone, Colette Winn, and Tili Boon Cuillé to my arguments. Similarly, at the University of Pittsburgh, Drew Armstrong and Chloé Hogg invited me to give one in a series of lectures on Versailles. I enjoyed talking both to them and their students, learning much from their complex approaches to French culture. In addition, I am grateful to both the STS group at Bar Ilan University and members of the Safra Center of the University of Tel Aviv who talked with me both formally and informally about modernity and inarticulacy, providing a rich opportunity for improving my arguments. Thanks particularly to Anat Leibler, Noah Efron, and Hagai Boas for setting up these meetings.

I am also grateful to members of the "Spicy City Crew": Lesley Stern, Jeffrey Minson, David and Gail Matlin, Jerry and Diane Rothenberg, and George Webb. Their ongoing support has been priceless, and their discussions about writing have made the difficult process of putting words on the page a lovely collective adventure. I am particularly grateful to Lesley and Jeffrey for also reading chapters for me when I was most worried about them, giving me useful feedback when I most needed it.

In addition, I would like to thank the Center for Advanced Study in the Behavioral Sciences for supporting me during the early stages of this project, and the University of California Humanities Research Institute (UCHRI) for funding of a joint project on Material Worlds and Social Life in which I worked on some of these chapters. I particularly want to thank Marian Feldman who organized an Object Agency working group at the Center for Advanced Study in the Behavioral Sciences (CASBS) and transformed it into the Material Worlds and Social Life project funded by the University of California Humanities Research Institute (UCHRI). The participants shaped my views of history, materiality, and modernity. They included not only Marian Feldman (as leader), but also (at various stages) Fred Turner, Karin Knorr-Cetina, Gina Neff, Kelly Gates, Barry Brown, Paula Findlen, Mark Peterson, Benjamin Porter, and Heghnar Watenpaugh.

Finally, I am grateful to my husband, Zachary Fisk, for his support. This book turned into a much bigger project than I had imagined, and I periodically floundered, trying to figure out what to do. When I hit an impasse, he simply brought me some wine, and started talking about some interesting book he was reading, getting me out of my troubled head. Heroism takes many forms, and his is the quiet, intelligent, and modest version.

PART ONE

HISTORY OF MODERN SOCIAL FORMS

CHAPTER ONE

Modern Selves and Fashion

In the 14th century, Europe was ravaged by the Black Death. Many cities affected by the early appearance of this plague lost 60 to 80 percent of their populations.[1] Groups that thought their piety had spared them soon learned that the disease would infect their towns, too. Families were devastated, and survivors were not sure how to go on. They could not live as they had before. They could not count on their inherited identities to mean anything.[2] Those who faced the new social landscape became modern social selves, inventing themselves and taking control of their lives in ways they had never imagined before. They helped to build a capitalist economy as they sought new opportunities and dreamt of new ways of being in the world. And merchants and artisans who made fortunes and fine reputations refused to accept their traditional subordination to nobles and the clergy, starting a revolution from below that never really stopped.

Men of commerce in Burgundy asserted their new sense of autonomy and importance both visibly and silently. They violated the implicit codes of dress meant to mark their low status. Only nobles and high members of the clergy were allowed to adorn themselves with red clothes, fine furs, refined cloth, and jewels. But Burgundian merchants and artisans started to cover themselves with this kind of finery—a breach of decorum that became possible after the unthinkable plague had devoured so many lives and tested so many limits.

The nobles, reasserting their traditional superiority, adopted new styles of dress, inventing new signs of noble standing. But the merchants simply followed their lead, and put on the new fashions. Merchants were the ones who brought the fine fabrics, furs, and precious stones to courts to sell to nobles, so they had access to the best. Nobles innovated,

---

[1] David Herlihy, *The Black Death and the Transformation of the West*. Samuel K. Cohn, Jr, editor (Cambridge, MA: Harvard University Press, 1997).

[2] George Huppert, *After the Black Death: A Social History of Early Modern Europe* (Bloomington: Indiana University Press, 2nd edition, 1998).

FIGURE 1.1 *Burgundian Fashion. Petrus Christus,* Portrait of a Young Girl, *1460*

merchants followed, and the result was the modern system of fashionable change: a pattern of innovation and imitation in dress that defined superiority and made clothing go out of style.[3]

Why should we care that the fashion system developed in 14th-century Burgundy? The simple answer is that it marked an important turning point in the development of modern culture. Fashion was the province of modern self-fashioning individuals who invented selves and lives as they went along. People who had lost their families, towns, and habits started to measure their worth by the lives they could create. They dreamt about the future in a way that had not made sense before. They began to recognize themselves as actors in history who could use their personal capabilities to create identities. Dress became a vehicle of personal formation and moral or social discipline (see Figure 1.1).

To understand this emergent modern self, and appreciate its radical break with the past, we need to begin by looking at the culture that preceded it. Only then can we appreciate the shift in identity and temporality in the wake of the Black Death.

MEDIEVAL IDENTITY

Before the 14th century, most people in Europe inhabited a relatively stable social order. They did not expect their lives to be radically different from the lives of their parents. Their social destinies were mainly set at birth by their family's social position. Their inner nature was constant, not something to develop; it was their soul, engaged in ongoing moral struggles against evil. Most people lived in small towns or villages where people knew them, and they knew who they were supposed to be.

The social hierarchy was comprised of three estates (the clergy, the nobility, and the third estate), each morally differentiated from the others by their relationship to God. People might change their fortunes by going into monasteries or convents, but the line between nobles and their inferiors was rigidly drawn. The clergy were keepers of God's word. Nobles were the political elite charged with exercising God's will on earth. Both mediated between God and men. Members of the third estate, on the other hand, were in charge of worldly things—tilling the earth, engaging in

---

[3] Chandra Mukerji, *From Graven Images: Patterns of Modern Materialism* (New York: Columbia University Press, 1983).

manufacture, trading in goods, or sailing the seas—which placed them in a different moral stratum.

As Natalie Zemon Davis has shown,[4] identities were not distinctly individual in such communities. Even as late as the 16th century, a peasant who claimed to be Martin Guerre "returned" to his village after many years at war, and was accepted by his wife, who was happy to have a good husband. Only later when issues of inheritance were raised did members of her family question this and prosecute the man for impersonating Guerre. In rural France, an identity was a matter of social recognition rather than individual attributes.

Life was at its core a cycle of birth, striving, joy, loss, and eventual death, and social life was organized around seasons, life cycles, fortunes, and Saints days. Good Christians learned that the earth was Creation, and that the children of Adam had to till the land, experiencing toil and suffering, as penance for Adam and Eve's sin. People faced the same moral duties, expecting events to recur, even if the weather and harvests could change; they imagined themselves caught on a wheel of fortune where personal aspirations did not make sense (see Figure 1.2).[5]

People living in the country in the Middle Ages did experience and seek some change, but stayed close in word if not deed to the moral imaginary of Christian values. They could be prosecuted as heretics if they had independent ideas, and many were.[6] But peasants and artisans were free to change their material circumstances, using the intelligence that God had given Adam. So, people invented new spinning wheels, wine presses, and plows. They also used waterpower in mills to make paper, tan hides, and grind grain. A number of towns in the countryside became manufacturing centers where mills supported the growth of industry. The rising power of Burgesses in some towns foreshadowed the growth of capitalist trade. But usury was still a sin in the eyes of the Church, and limited profits.[7]

Nobles shared with members of the third estate the Christian belief that social life was stable, and social standing was reproduced across generations. To assure that domains

FIGURE 1.2 *Cyclical Time and the Wheel of Fortune. Dürer,* Wheel of Fortune, *in Sebastian Brant,* Ship of Fools, *1498*

[4] Natalie Zemon Davis, *The Return of Martin Guerre* (Cambridge, MA: Harvard University Press, 1983).

[5] Marc Bloch, *French Rural History: An Essay on its Basic Characteristics,* trans. Janet Sondheimer (London: Routledge and Kegan Paul, 1978).

[6] Carlo Ginzburg, *The Cheese and the Worms: The Cosmos of a Sixteenth-Century Miller,* trans. John and Anne Tedeschi (Baltimore: Johns Hopkins University Press, 1992).

[7] Fritz Rörig, *The Medieval Town* (Berkeley and Los Angeles: University of California Press, 1967).

and offices remained in noble hands, noble women married noble men, or went to a convent so they would not produce (legitimate) children. In this way, they tried to make the passage of noble rights and lands seem as cyclical and inevitable as birth and death.[8]

Artisans, for their part, were organized into guilds or similar occupational associations designed to assure the reproduction of traditional skills. They taught practical knowledge by apprenticeship. Often sons apprenticed in the family trade, and married daughters of artisans. So, family and work habits for artisans assured that their social identities were also reproduced.[9]

Marc Bloch[10] argued that the increase of trade in the 14th and 15th centuries helped break down the isolation and agricultural economy of feudal Europe, allowing modern life to develop outside of major cities. Trade allowed people to dream of new places to go, new things to acquire and sell, new profits, and new lives. But it was the plague, killing so many people that it made old lives impossible, that forced people to reinvent themselves.

THE BLACK DEATH

The Black Death came across the Eurasian steppes where trade routes connected China, Russia, and Iran to the Mediterranean. At this intersection of worlds, trade had been increasing, creating wider and more profitable flows of goods, people, and ideas. But the plague had become endemic to the region, and started to move with the goods.

Sailors from Genoa apparently boarded a ship to Italy with merchandise brought across the steppes, carrying the fleas or rats and fleas. The crew became infected, but a few managed to get back to Italy alive, bringing the disease into Europe. In most cities in Southern and Western Europe, an average of 60 percent of the population died, although in some places the death rate was closer to 90 or 95 percent. It struck cities first and foremost, so elites that had country estates fled for their lives. But the plague turned out to be even more lethal in parts of the countryside where there were more rats per capita, living off of the fields. If the fleas reached them, the plague was fierce. Sometimes, unpopulated areas between rural towns and estates stopped the movement of the fleas and rats; other times, the disease, following river trade, stopped at the river sources on hillsides, never crossing down to the next valley. But in most places, the fleas found carriers to keep the disease agent moving.[11] The rats and fleas moved slowly but relentlessly from Genoa and

---

[8] Chandra Mukerji, "Jurisdiction, Inscriptions and State Formation," *Theory and Society* (2011), 40(3): 223–45.

[9] Huppert, *After the Black Death*, chapter 3; Natalie Zemon Davis, *Society and Culture in Early Modern France* (Stanford: Stanford University Press, 1975). Robert Darnton, *The Great Cat Massacre, and Other Episodes in French Cultural History* (New York: Basic Books, 1999).

[10] See Bloch, *French Rural History*, chapter 3.

[11] See John Kelly, *The Great Mortality: An Intimate History of the Black Death, the Most Devastating Plague of All Time* (New York: Harper Collins, 2005), chapter 11. See also, Herlihy, *The Black Death and the Transformation of the West*, chapter 2.

other parts of Southern Europe north through Switzerland, France, England, Burgundy, and Germany—then turning east into Russia.[12]

Death could come in a day or two. And the growing numbers of dead and ill vividly demonstrated that the future would not always be like the past. The plague undermined the authority of the Church that was helpless to stop it. The plague made a mockery of the moral hierarchy of feudal ranks, too, since rich, poor, sinners, and saints all died or lived in apparently random patterns. If the plague attacked men for their sins, no one seemed closer to God than anyone else. In this way, the Black Death rattled the temporal, social, and moral foundations of the feudal order.[13]

It was called the Black Death for the black marks it left on its victims, the grim results of its visits, and the sin it was supposed to embody and destroy. Europe was being punished, people argued. Worried communities found scapegoats to attack. Groups in Switzerland and Germany, among others, burned families or even whole communities of Jews, convinced that their sinful ways were the cause of God's wrath. Jews were associated with trade, and usury—the source of the disease. But these massacres did nothing to the rats or fleas. The plague was impersonal, silent, and deadly—like famine but worse.[14]

The pace of social change was startling. Relatives that people talked to in the morning could be dead by night, and towns that had been populated became empty as most died and the rest fled. Family members, neighbors, friends, laborers, apprentices, soldiers, sailors, artisans, lawyers, notaries, monks, and heirs to the throne all died.

The survivors were cast swiftly and unceremoniously into a different world. No one could reverse what had happened. Being modern was not a matter of choice, but rather a trial of character and a way to proceed. The living *had* to forge new identities to face a future they could barely imagine. The losses created a rift between feudal ways of life and modern selves. A small pathogen on a flea on a rat brought about the painful, howling birth of the modern world.

Only in the north, notably in Burgundy—where cold weather reduced the load of fleas and the population was healthier—did the plague have less of an effect. Sandwiched between France and Germany, Burgundy was only a small duchy, but it controlled land from the Atlantic port at Bruges down to the Rhône River that

FIGURE 1.3 *Images of the Plague in Popular Culture. Michael Wolgemut,* Dance of Death, *1493*

---

[12] Kelly, *The Great Mortality*, chapter 11.

[13] William H. McNeill, *Plagues and Peoples* (New York: Anchor Books, 1976), chapter 4.

[14] Kelly, *The Great Mortality*, chapter 10.

FIGURE 1.4 *Burgundy and Lands Under Control of Charles "the Bold"*

flowed to the Mediterranean. So, it linked the two great trading systems. Bruges lost only about 15 to 25 percent of the population to the plague, too, so it still had the people and skills to maintain trade. The Mediterranean trade plummeted, and Burgundy became rich.[15]

Luxuries from all over the world flowed through the duchy, the most important being textiles. These were the primary items of long-distance exchange, and the basis for the fashion system. Textiles included ribbons and laces, and large bolts of brocades, embroideries, silks, wools, and velvets.[16]

The pursuit of wealth and luxury still remained troubling to many. Images of the Wheel of Fortune (Figure 1.2) and the Dance of Death (Figure 1.3) in the 15th and 16th centuries ridiculed the pretenses of survivors, depicting pitiful and deluded characters that thought too much of themselves and were afflicted by God for their stupidity. Only fools would deny that their fate was in the hands of God. But life had changed, and the elites in Burgundy who profited from the collective disaster could not go back to the past if they wanted to. So, they put on new clothes, expressed pious gratitude for their blessings, and took control of their own moral character and fate.

MODERN SUBJECTIVITY

On what basis can we argue that the fashion system marked a shift in subjectivity? How do we know that people were trying to fashion new identities when they put on new clothes? We could see fashion simply as a response to trade and the availability of goods. But clothes in Burgundy were used for addressing questions about moral worth—issues being discussed by Italian humanists who had also survived the plague and tried to understand its implications. Those in Bruges and Florence alike recognized that the future would no longer be like the past; they examined their inner being, and took responsibility for their own moral standing.

Petrarch, the most celebrated of the 14th-century humanists, understood himself as a historical actor who would be judged in the future for his conduct in the present. Anticipating his own mortality, he eerily wrote to posterity, describing himself as "a poor mortal like yourself, neither very exalted in my origin, nor, on the other hand, of the most humble

---

[15] Kelly, *The Great Mortality*, chapters 11–12.

[16] Mukerji, *From Graven Images*.

birth." He was not socially important, but he had transformative ideas about human souls and lives. The point of life, he suggested, was to gain the self-knowledge to be able to act well in facing the future, understanding that you would be judged by history and not just your peers. Writing and reading worked for Petrarch as clothes did for merchants in Burgundy, serving as tools of inner transformation and social formation.[17]

Petrarch lived as a modern man, too, reinventing himself and his life multiple times after the plague. He had been serving at the court of the exiled pope in Avignon when the Black Death arrived. The pope fled the city rather than risking his life to care for his flock, so Petrarch left, condemning his patron's venality and weakness. He started to look for a new patron worthy of his counsel, and continued moving because it was hard to find such a person.

Boccaccio[18] was another humanist who survived the plague, and wrote about it in the *Decameron*. He treated it as a time of moral reckoning, personal introspection, and reflection on accepted social ranks and traditions.

In the *Decameron*, a group of young people flee to an estate outside Florence while the plague is raging in the city.[19] The young refugees enjoy a good life in the country with food, wine, and walks in the garden, but they also reflect on ways of living now that human life seems so fleeting. Every day, each member of the group tells a story to entertain the rest. They playfully flirt with one another, tell some bawdy tales, and revel in the pleasure of laughter. They embrace their humanity and what life is left for them. But they focus on the misadventures of people with poor character, the cleverness of those who use their wits to protect their integrity, and the contradictions between the social hierarchy and inner qualities of people.[20]

In the first story—one particularly important for thinking about the rise of the fashion system—an Italian merchant needs a representative to go to Burgundy to conduct business for him. The Burgundians are clever and can be duplicitous, he thinks, so although he is an honest man, the merchant selects a con man to represent him. This agent is to stay at the house of a friend, but soon after arriving, falls gravely ill. The host becomes worried. He does not want a man of such low morals to die in his house and debase the reputation of his family, but he also does not want to throw out a dying man. The bedridden visitor tells him not to worry, but to send a monk to administer the last rites. The monk arrives, and the con man confesses so artfully that he appears to the monk

---

[17] See Karl Enenkel, Betsy de Jong-Crane, and Peter Liebgrets, *Modelling the Individual* (Amsterdam: Rodopi, 1998); Francesco Petrach, *Familial Letters*. See, for example, "The Ascent of Mount Ventoux," where he analyzed his inner desires with care. And for his reflections on love, see Petrach, *The Complete Canzoniere*, translated and annotated by A. S. Kline (Poetry in Translation, 2001).

[18] Giovanni Boccaccio, *The Decameron*, trans. Mark Musa and Peter Bondanella (New York: Norton, 1977). See also the online version: www.brown.edu/Departments/Italian_Studies/dweb/texts/

[19] Boccaccio, *The Decameron*, pp. 1–17.

[20] Boccaccio, *The Decameron*, pp. 1–17.

as a most modest and holy man. The monk is so impressed that he gets permission from his superior to let the dying man be buried in the monastery's cemetery. The con man dies, is buried, and becomes so legendary for his virtue that his grave becomes an object of pilgrimage.[21]

Hearing this story, the young people outside Florence have a good laugh. But they recognize, too, the failure of the Church to maintain moral order. They agree that each person has a moral responsibility for his or her acts. Even a con man can care for a kind host. The problem in life, they suggest, is to gain the intellectual ability and moral discipline to live in an uncertain world with integrity.

Clearly, Boccaccio did not think the Burgundians were particularly virtuous; neither did he think that the duchy was free from disease. But in the wake of the plague, Burgundian elites wanted to embody the virtues praised in the *Decameron*, and used clothes to display this.

BURGUNDIAN FASHION AND MORAL WORTH

The fashion system began in Burgundy when merchants and nobles who benefitted from the plague started competing with one another through clothing, while grappling with the moral peril of their success. They wanted to assert their importance, but they also wanted to understand themselves as moral actors, so they used modest and simple clothes of high quality in their fashions.[22]

Why did Burgundian elites turn to clothes to build new identities? Partly, it was because they had access to trade goods, and everything else had changed. But in addition, dress was inarticulate, so when low-ranking beneficiaries of trade in Burgundy violated norms of conduct by dressing above their station, they did not criticize the rules or question the basis of the social ranks. Putting on fine goods was a way to express the change in local fortunes. And they dressed modestly to look worthy of their unearned blessings.

Rogier van der Weyden's *Portrait of a Lady* (Figure 1.5) illustrates the basic features of Burgundian fashion. The elegant, restrained woman is adorned in well-made but simple garments. The modesty of her pose exemplifies the kind of good character that the young people in the *Decameron* admired. Her linen headdress is plain, but the fabric is fine enough to see through and carefully draped over her hair with a cap decorated with gold. She covers her breasts with a linen undergarment, too, a bourgeois method of not only protecting clothes, but also suggesting an inner purity (compare to Figure 1.6).

---

[21] Boccaccio, *The Decameron*, pp. 18–28.

[22] This form of self-fashioning is understood best through figured world theory, the projection of cultural imaginaries, and the use of material activities to make them real. See Dorothy Holland, William S. Lachicotte, Jr, Debra Skinner, and Carole Cain, *Identity and Agency in Cultural Worlds* (Cambridge, MA: Harvard University, 1998).

FIGURE 1.5 *Modesty and Piety in Burgundian Fashion.*
Rogier van der Weyden, Portrait of a Lady, *1460*

FIGURE 1.6 *The Modest Dress of the Man who made*
Burgundy Rich and Powerful. Rogier van der Weyden, Philip
the Good, *1450*

Van der Weyden's portrait of Philip the Good (Figure 1.6)—the man who unified Burgundy and made it a great trading center—presents him as unpretentious. The Duke is wearing a simple tunic with wide shoulders, looking away from the viewer, and holding his hands up in prayer. His taste is subtle. He seems to be wearing soft wool, and the slight curve of his hat speaks to its softness, too. Philip is not wrapped in the red or purple fabrics permitted for nobles; he only uses a modest amount of gold jewelry to mark his standing. He also wears linen under his coat, suggesting cleanliness and inner virtue. His clothes are not tools of calculating self-aggrandizement, but rather marks of constraint and inner discipline.

In contrast, Jan van Eyck, an artist at the court of Philip the Good, paints himself wearing a red turban, the color representing the blood of Christ traditionally used to mark the clergy or nobility (Figure 1.7). The rest of his appearance is modest, but his use of red to assert an inner nobility of spirit illustrates how non-nobles were starting to use forms of dress to make new kinds of social claims.

FIGURE 1.7 *The Use of Red Fabric in a Painter's Self Portrait. Jan van Eyck,* Portrait of a Man in a Turban, *1433*

The fashionable elites of Burgundy dressed less according to who they were than what kind of person they hoped to become. Clothes for them became a means of engineering new selves from the outside. Becoming fashionable was not just a way to claim social importance, then, but to claim moral authority and standing without noble blood.

ITALIAN FASHION AND THE DISTANT SELF

Fashion did not remain centered in Burgundy, and dreams of what modern selves could or should be began to shift. Dressing well remained a way of claiming inner nobility, but what constituted noble character took new forms as centers of power moved. Fashion followed patterns of global power and wealth, and modern selves claimed new qualities of superiority.

The center of fashionable taste moved first from Burgundy to the Italian city-states in the 15th and 16th centuries when trade picked up in the Mediterranean. The losses of the Black Death had concentrated wealth significantly in Italy, but also hollowed people out emotionally, leaving them struggling to reconfigure their identities and develop new ways of being with each other. With so much to invent, people became inventive. This was the Renaissance, and a creative moment. But with ties to others now more calculated and political, nobility acquired new traits: rationality, distance, objectivity, learning, taste, studied etiquette, and strong will. Capitalist ventures and political life thrived in this culture, and so did fashion. Those who followed fashion managed their public demeanor seriously for political effect.

Fashion was particularly vibrant because wealth had been concentrated in so few hands after the plague that money mattered, and bourgeois elites were powerful. Bankers as well as merchants vied with nobles for public esteem. There was more gold to amass, more capital to put to work, more enterprises to fund, more luxuries to enjoy, and more opportunities to improve one's fortune. Italian manners and courtly graces were elaborated to new heights to mark nobility of spirit with performances of superiority. And the rules were outlined in courtesy books to address the needs of the upwardly mobile.[23] Machiavelli[24] showed that political calculation was important to public life, too. In this context, members of Italian courts claimed nobility with reason and expressed their standing with calculated

---

[23] Norbert Elias, *The Civilizing Process* (New York: Pantheon Books, 1982), vol. I.
[24] Niccolò Machiavelli, *The Prince*, trans. Donno (New York: Bantam, 1966).

performances of the self that relied on theatrical displays of authority more than the modesty and piety of Burgundian nobles. Renaissance elites performed on the public stage, playing the social roles expected of them, but also displaying an independence of will and reason that defined their character as strong and worthy.

The portraits by Bronzino are particularly revealing of the conception of noble dignity in Italian fashion—the outer charm and inner reticence and calculation. The clothing of his subjects is always impeccably elegant and charmingly attractive, but it is matched by distant, calculating eyes. His subjects seem lost in grief and thought.

Bronzino's *Portrait of Eleanor of Toledo* (Figure 1.8) shows her to be both removed and on stage. She is depicted as a pretty, fashionable, and powerful young mother. Seated by her son, she wears a bodice decorated with a pomegranate, a common image on Italian brocades that stood for fertility and sexuality because of the fruit's many seeds. She enacts the role of mother, but shows no particular warmth or affection to her son, Giovanni, other than loosely holding him with her arm. There is no love in her eyes, or much interest in human contact. Eleanor claims wealth and high standing with her rich brocade and multiple strands of jewelry typical of Italian fashion. She has layered Renaissance sleeves, too,

FIGURE 1.8 *Charm and Cold Calculation in the Dress and Demeanor of Italian Elites. Bronzino,* Eleanor of Toledo and Son, *1545*

that seem to suggest a distinction between outer and inner selves. The slits are narrow and tied shut, but allow others to see fabric beneath the main dress. It is different than the brocade, suggesting an inner self that is veiled—just what we recognize in Eleanor's eyes. The charm of her clothing is juxtaposed to the drained but fierce quality of her expression. She is held in place by her clothing and child, but she also holds the viewer with her gaze, suggesting a strong inner character that is carefully regulated.

Bronzino often uses books, glasses, and classical references in his portraits to display his subjects' interest in learning and rational pursuits. The girl in Figure 1.9, for example, is reading a book and wears jewelry in her hair like ancient Greek women. Her necklace with its large pendant is reminiscent of Roman jewelry that included pendants of large precious and semi-precious stones. Her knowledge of classical culture is claimed with her attire as well as her book.

Men were similarly extravagant in their clothing and cold in their expressions in Bronzino's portraits. Being thoughtful, intelligent, removed, and fiercely independent seemed to be the hallmark of fashionable Renaissance men and women.

This conception of the person was not just an invention of Bronzino. Andrea Solario also shows in his portrait of Charles II d'Amboise (Figure 1.10) a man who is serious,

FIGURE 1.9 *The Fashion for Books and Classical Knowledge in Italian Dress. Bronzino,* Portrait of a Girl with a Book, *1545*

FIGURE 1.10 *Expressions of Inner Character and Italian Fashion. Andrea Solario,* Charles II d'Amboise, *c. 1507*

fierce, and well appointed, with a pin in his hat and jewelry on his body to display his wealth and power. His clothing is layered with brocades, furs, silks, and woolens. He also mixes jewels with shells, and gold with red to produce a very dramatic vision of taste and superiority. Solario also places Charles in the landscape, suggesting that his property helps make him a man of power.

Charles d'Amboise (Figure 1.10) stares intently and coldly out from the painting at the viewer, displaying himself to be a man of strong character whose careful self-governance in dress implies his personal capacity to govern others.

If the Burgundians invented costumes for displaying gratitude for their survival in fashionable dress, the Italians developed clothing that embodied the wealth, intelligence, and cold character they had developed in response to the plague. They dressed as strong, willful, and resourceful survivors who were building better worlds to replace the ones that had been lost, using the material powers and creative capacities left to them. All the people in these portraits use artifacts to try to embody a cultural imaginary of the modern self as a rational actor capable of governing wisely both the world and self.

SPANISH FASHION AND THE CHRISTIAN WARRIOR

When the center of fashion shifted to Spain in the 16th century, clothing started to change again, following a new logic of self-fashioning. Now dress was costuming for Christian soldiers, pursuing empire in the name of the Catholic Church. These warriors carried and flaunted the destructive power of modernity, tearing down other cultures to allow the Spanish Empire to spread God's word and Spain's mission around the world. The clothing became militaristic and disciplining, putting pride and honor above economic calculation. But displays of wealth mattered, too. The Spanish used masses of pearls and jewels to testify to the reach and wealth of the empire.

Spanish fashions were characterized by the proud posture enforced by upper body armor or corselets shaped like the armor, holding the body erect. Ruffs around the neck held the head up even higher, creating a haughty appearance. The armor ended just above the genitals. Below, women wore skirts, and men wore leggings, short pants, and codpieces to cover and emphasize their genitals. The result was an image of military discipline (and masculinity for men) for the leaders of the Holy Roman Empire (see Figure 1.11).

Charles V of Spain, heir to the Habsburg monarchy, gained control over the trading centers of Burgundy as well as parts of Italy, and set up a colonial empire in the New World that spread the faith to heathens, and assured a flow of bullion that he used to fund military campaigns. In his portrait by Seisenegger (Figure 1.11) Charles V displays his standing and the honor of his position with broad shoulders, puffed sleeves, fur collar, and large codpiece over his private parts.

Spain was the only kingdom in Europe with a standing military and it was staunchly Catholic, too, so it should be no surprise that Spanish elites dressed as proud soldiers of the Church. Charles V's successor, Philip II, for example, was explicitly a religious crusader, and dressed the part. That is why he wore armor to express his character and power in a portrait by Titian (Figure 1.12). His version of nobility was dedicated to moral purpose and personal discipline, extending the power of the Catholic Church as an act of self-fashioning.

Women did not wear armor, but they wore its equivalent, the corselet, to exercise the same level of discipline over their bodies as men. They also dressed with high ruffs and broad shoulders, but they wore masses of jewelry, displaying the power of the Empire.

FIGURE 1.11 *Masculinity and Discipline in Spanish Fashion. Jacob Seisenegger,* Portrait of Emperor Charles V with a Dog, *1532*

FIGURE 1.13 *The Disciplined Body of Women Defenders of the Faith in Spanish Fashion. Juan Pantoja de la Cruz,* Isabel de Valois, *1565*

FIGURE 1.12 *Military Prowess and Armor as Fashion in Philip II's Spain. Titian,* Portrait of Philip II, *1550–1*

Philip II's wife, Isabel de Valois (Figure 1.13), is a moral crusader in her own way. She displays her modesty as a good Catholic woman by concealing her head with a hat, holding her upper body stiff with a corselet, and using a farthingale or *verdugado* under her skirt. This gives the lower part of her costume a conical shape minimally affected by the curves of her body. She embodies Christian virtue.

The sleeves on Isabel de Valois are particularly interesting and indicative of Spanish fashion. They have two layers like Italian Renaissance sleeves, but the inner layer is fully visible. Her inner character is presented as open to public view. And because her inner sleeve is red and gold, representing the blood of Christ, she is characterized as essentially moral. Her outer garment is black, the color worn by most of the clergy and the favorite color for Spanish fashion, suggesting her religious bent. The whole costume, then, uses color to indicate in Philip II's wife an inner nobility and a moral character appropriate for a defender of the faith and leader of empire.

Spanish dress in all its forms, in other words, was a costume for moral crusaders—a way of disciplining bodies to serve Christianity and to make visible the moral foundations of the Spanish Empire. Following this fashion was still a form of self-fashioning, but one in which obedience to a higher power and acting as an agent of God were the most noble of virtues.

DUTCH FASHION AND CONSUMER CULTURE

When Holland revolted against Spain and established the Dutch Republic in the early 17th century, the Netherlands became the center of commerce and fashion. In this Dutch "Golden Age," commercial values—the pleasures and dangers of consumption—dominated aesthetic life, including dress. As the commercial leaders of Europe, the Dutch had access to the luxuries of the world. And in this bourgeois society, more people were consumers and followed fashion. But their access to goods also made Dutch people worry about the moral dangers of wanting too much. So, self-fashioning in the Netherlands was a matter of negotiating the moral risks of consumption while relishing things.[25]

Dutch fashion was liberal like Dutch society; people had choices. Pious members of Reformed religions wore simple, black, comfortable clothes. They demonstrated their moral commitments to living according to the Bible. Members of the noble families of the Netherlands and their followers, in contrast, wore the lighter colors, laces, ribbons, and feathers, and some wore soft wide hats or Cavalier-style hats with feathers. They took up many decorative items rare in the Spanish court like ribbons and large lace collars, and they also wore clothes with more sloping shoulders, a looser fit, and softer collars (Figures 1.14, 1.15, and 1.16). Their clothes were ways of being comfortable in the world, but also a reminder not to become too vain and proud.

Figure 1.14 *Bourgeois Fashion in the Netherlands. Bartholomeus van der Helst, Abraham del Court and His Wife Maria de Keerssegieter, 1654*

---

[25] Simon Schama, *The Embarrassment of Riches: An Interpretation of Dutch Culture in the Golden Age* (New York: Knopf, 1987).

FIGURE 1.15 *Noble Fashions in the Netherlands. Anthony Van Dyck,* Lady Charlotte Butkens and Her Son, c. *1631*

Dutch noble women still wore some jewelry, and used corselets, but the corselets were looser to allow stomachs to bulge. Women also lowered their necklines so they could move and breathe, and decked themselves out with layer upon layer of fine fabrics, using their bodies for displays of cosmopolitanism and luxury (Figure 1.15).

In Dutch life, many men assumed work-based uniforms that demonstrated their affiliations with corporations, guilds, or trading associations, displaying their obligations to others. We can see an example in Rembrandt's painting of the *Syndics of the Draper's Guild* (Figure 1.16).

Families dressed alike, too, presenting themselves as a moral unit with shared commitments to beauty and modesty. Gender differences were nonetheless marked in Dutch clothing as they had been in Spanish dress, with pants for men and skirts for women. The gender ideal in the Netherlands, however, shifted as the Dutch developed a culture of domesticity. In principle, in this trading nation, men went to sea while women stayed at home. So, women were expected to be mothers, and women's fashions often had low necks and bulging stomachs, celebrating female fertility in a way quite alien to Eleanor of Toledo (Figure 1.8).

Dutch fashion negotiated commercial culture and its bad moral effects by making dress increasingly a form of collective commitment that kept individuals in check. Individuals chose to fashion collective identities, and tie their futures to those of others. Fashion became a system of social conformity, but also emphasized personal comfort as a way of balancing the pleasures of consumerism with the moral dangers of materialism and personal vanity in the pursuit of capitalist profits and consumer pleasures.

FRENCH FASHION AND THE THEATER OF POWER

Enforcing stylistic constraints on those who lived at court, the king of France made Versailles a center of splendor, luxury, and political discipline. As fashionable elites throughout Europe embraced the luxurious tastes of the French court, fashion in France became a medium for displaying hierarchy within the nobility, and projecting the king's vision of French grandeur. French dress was not just costuming for court life, but also for claiming degrees of nobility on the world stage. French fashions were as excessive and dramatic as

FIGURE 1.16 *Dutch Dress for Merchants and Artisans. Rembrandt,* Syndics of the Draper's Guild, *1662*

the Sun King—part of the theater of power at Versailles. The nobles who joined the court at Versailles were as calculating, haughty, and distant as their counterparts in the Renaissance courts of Italy, but they projected an even greater degree of political commitment with their clothes. Like Spanish fashions, French clothes for men were showy versions of military uniforms. But like Dutch dress, French fashions expressed social affiliations through strict conformity to court attire. The uniformity at Versailles had its economic usefulness. The administration built factories to manufacture fashionable textiles, stimulating industry through leadership in fashion.[26]

The point was to organize collective ambitions and desires through clothes, defining what France was by what it could become. Dreams of classical revival circulated through Versailles, and were invested in images of Louis IV as a hero or god in the classical mold (see Figure 1.17). To fit the part of a superior person, Louis XIV wore high-heeled shoes to seem taller than he was and to emphasize the muscles of his dancer legs. Fashion was an extension of these serious games of political make-believe.

---

[26] William Sewell, "The Empire of Fashion and the Rise of Capitalism in 18th-century France," *Past and Present* (2010), 206(1): 81–120; Chandra Mukerji, *Territorial Ambitions and the Gardens of Versailles* (Cambridge: Cambridge University Press, 1997), chapters 3 and 5.

FIGURE 1.18 *French Military Masculinity in Fashion, Luxury, and Seriousness. Claude Lefèbvre,* Louis XIV, *c. 1670*

FIGURE 1.17 *The Theatrical Framing of Louis XIV as a Classical-Style Hero. Hyacinthe Rigaud,* Portrait of Louis XIV, King of France, *1701*

The king Louis XIV developed a French style of military masculinity, defining France as heir to Rome and its imperial glory. The "Court Habit" for men resembled a military uniform, with a sash across the chest, loose pants to the knee, leggings, and high heels—everything decorated with laces and feathers worthy of heroes (see Figure 1.18). There was no contradiction between fashionable luxury and masculinity. Love of finery in the French court was not accompanied by the anxiety about moral corruption that the Dutch felt. Quite the contrary, luxury implied imperial wealth and global reach. So, there was no limit to the opulence of French fashion since it reflected the king's imperial ambitions (see Figure 1.19).

Women as well as men were expected to maintain the discipline of good soldiers. So, they wore stomachers—relatives of corsets—like armor to maintain a regal posture. Famously, Louis XIV had his granddaughter wear full fashionable attire to accompany him on a journey when she was pregnant, making her miscarry.[27]

---

[27] Mukerji, *Territorial Ambitions and the Gardens of Versailles,* pp. 239–41.

Like Spanish women, French ladies at court wore farthingales under their skirts, but they had low-cut bodices with delicate scarves over their breasts that were both revealing and concealing in an evocative way. They projected a vision of female beauty comparable to that of Italian fashion, but they wore French brocades and laces that resembled the design of French garden beds. In this way, French fashion linked political territory and bodies through style.

Fashion in France became a tool of noble subordination to the state and king, but nobles were still modern selves, choosing to connect their identities to that of the French state and pursuing personal futures around collective ambitions. They used clothing for conveying loyalties, making alliances, and expressing nobility through distinctly French tastes.[28] Dress became a way of fashioning a self for political gain.

FASHIONABLE DRESS AND MODERN SELVES

Modern individuals stepped away from the horror of the plague, and started to fashion selves and new social worlds using dress to express and explore what modern selves could be. Their desire for luxury goods stimulated trade and the growth of capitalism. And imported textiles gave them tools for self-fashioning, asserting identities against the grief of lost lives. In the absence of guidelines of how to be themselves, they performed their identities, improvising roles and learning what was possible to do. Fashion became costume, too, that put social identities in play. And with it, powerful elites asserted the importance of taste as a measure of inner nobility, linking social hierarchy to the world of goods.[29]

FIGURE 1.19 *Fashionable Attire for Women at Court. Marie Thérèse de Bourbon*, Princesse de Conti, c. *1690*

---

[28] Mukerji, *Territorial Ambitions and the Gardens of Versailles*, pp. 239–41.

[29] Pierre Bourdieu, *Distinction: A Social Critique of the Judgment of Taste*, trans. Richard Nice (London: Routledge and Kegan Paul, 1984).

CHAPTER TWO

COMMUNITIES OF STRANGERS AND INFRASTRUCTURE

Modern selves not only invented new ways of dressing, but also agitated for other changes. Given a shortage of labor after the plague, peasants started rebellions, rejecting their servitude and clamoring into the 16th century for new privileges and freedoms. Critics of the Church proliferated, too, encouraging Martin Luther in the early 16th century to post his critiques of the Church and start the Reformation. The Spanish, hoping to purify their faith and land, expelled the Jews in the 15th century and forced Moors to convert in the 16th century. Communities that had been held together with collective traditions were being destroyed—mainly due to religious divides.[1]

Max Weber[2] described the modern ethos embedded in Protestant (mainly Calvinist) conceptions of the person. The Protestant Ethic was not a set of theological commitments, but rather a cultural imaginary of moral struggle that individuals used to think about and improvise new lives. Members of the Reformed faiths gave up their dependence on priests and saints, and directed their devotion to the Bible and what they could learn of God's Word. Eschewing the comfort of institutional authority and ritual practices of forgiveness, Calvinists codified for believers a form of modern anxiety about the future. God held individuals responsible for their moral actions, and determined their moral destiny without letting them know their fates. So, people had to act without sure knowledge of their future, finding their moral dignity in the conduct of their lives, and guessing their moral standing by their worldly successes.

Weber argued that this cultural imaginary spawned capitalism by giving people reason to value personal, worldly achievement. But it also spawned a different kind of community—a community of believers who lived in dispersed places. This was a modern

---

[1] Peter Burke, *Popular Culture in Early Modern Europe* (London: Temple Smith, 1978).
[2] Max Weber, *Protestant Ethic and the Spirit of Capitalism*, trans. Talcott Parsons (New York: Scribners, 1958).

community, an imagined community in Benedict Anderson's terms,[3] providing a sense of belonging with minimal mutual obligations. It was a community based on dreams of shared similarities and built with an infrastructure of books. Reformers sought salvation by reading and careful study of the Bible.

In rejecting the past along with the Catholic Church, converts to the Reformed faiths dreamt of creating better lives. Their aspirations for a purified Christianity joined them to others who shared the same dream, but also produced intolerance toward the Catholic Church that Reformers defamed. Catholics, on the other hand, dreamt of retaking all of Europe, using military might as well as theology to regain control of those they had ruled previously. Communities were born and torn apart in the resulting violence. The social order did not crumble completely along with the bones of those that had died in the plague, but the cultural foundations of collective life were riddled with fissures. In this context, people sought new means of building communities with strangers—either to consolidate new beliefs or to exclude those holding onto tradition.

Social antagonisms and intolerance had certainly been part of European culture prior to this time. But the modern sense that things could be different created dreams along with hatred and contempt for those who did not entertain the same possibilities. Jews had been objects of attack by Christians for centuries, peasants had been mistreated by nobles, and heretics had been tortured and burned by the Church. But now intolerance was different, splintering Christianity itself, and the cultural foundations of local communities whose popular life had revolved around the Church. The question was how new communities of faith could develop, and how the differences among them could be bridged.

Infrastructures were used for building modern communities of strangers, creating social worlds[4] around shared practices. Why infrastructure? It was impersonal, limiting obligations to others. What infrastructures? Both urban and intellectual infrastructures. Urban infrastructure supported common ways of city life. Books linked people through shared ideas and reading practices. Those who used the same infrastructure for the same purposes did not have to know each other to belong to the same community. Even as strangers, they were connected by the objects and activities that distinguished them from others.[5]

The turn to infrastructures to shape new forms of community was not new to the 16th and 17th centuries. Cities were already being redesigned in the 15th century with better battlements to protect citizens, geometrical patterns of streets to support human reason, and ports and bridges to support trade. In Renaissance city-states, towns were

---

[3] Benedict Anderson, *Imagined Communities: Reflections on the Origins and Spread of Nationalism* (London: Verso, 1983).

[4] Howard Becker, *Art Worlds* (Berkeley: University of California Press, 1982); Susan Leigh Star, "The Ethnography of Infrastructure," *American Behavioral Scientist* (1999) 43(3): 377–91.

[5] Intellectual infrastructures created shared practices of knowing. See Karin Knorr-Cetina, *Epistemic Cultures* (Cambridge, MA: Harvard University Press, 1999); Jennifer A. Jordan, *Structures of Memory: Understanding Urban Change in Berlin and Beyond* (Stanford: Stanford University Press, 2006).

given new amenities like public art, plazas, markets, and cathedrals to become centers of faith, politics, trade, and manufacture.[6]

Printed books were already serving as intellectual infrastructures, too. Publishing houses in major cities in the 15th century had become centers of Humanist thought, changing ideas about the past and the future. But in the 16th century, printed books laid the foundation for Reformed faiths as independent reading of the Bible became key.[7]

Communities of strangers were modern because they were impersonal, built with weak ties, and put fewer constraints on members. They united people around shared activities without deep mutual obligations. The fashion system had already built a community of strangers around clothes. Bridges and books simply added to the repertoire of ways modern individuals coordinated their lives, and developed a sense of belonging.

As Granovetter has noted,[8] many communities based on weak ties grew with capitalism and its infrastructure of roads, harbors, bridges, warehouses, and exchanges. Merchants and seamen, carters and artisans, soldiers and shipbuilders were bound together with common amenities and dreams of amassing fortunes or building empires through capitalism. Members of trading communities shared practical knowledge because they did similar things. Crews from ships that did not necessarily know each other could nonetheless talk about the ports they visited, and the goods they saw traded there. They had little need for deep personal knowledge, and had limited obligations to one another. Goods only needed to be properly made, transported carefully, and delivered where needed. Objects became nodes in social networks, helping hold together trading communities that were both impersonal and practical.

These modern communities of strangers were quite unlike the intense communities of inhabitants in medieval villages and towns built around common traditions of family, work, and popular culture. Isolated rural communities were products of enduring face-to-face contacts, shared agricultural concerns, deep knowledge of one another, and a calendar of saints' days. Modern communities, on the other hand, replaced face-to-face interaction with face-to-object relations, allowing them to be multi-sited as well as more impersonal. For merchants engaged in global trade, strangers, ports, and artifacts halfway around the world could be more important than neighbors.

Communities of strangers were necessarily bounded in spite of their inclusiveness. There were only certain people in a given trading corporation, only some elites were fashionable, a limited number of writers were accepted as true scholars, and only some people going to sea were treated as real seamen. The boundaries of the communities were useful for building trust—a necessary ingredient in communities of weak ties.

---

[6] Helen Rosenau, *The Ideal City: Its Architectural Evolution in Europe* (New York: Methuen, 1982).

[7] Alberto Manguel, *A History of Reading* (London: Penguin, 1996); Elizabeth Eisenstein, *The Printing Press as an Agent of Change: Communication and Cultural Transformation in Early Modern Europe* (Cambridge: Cambridge University Press, 1979), vols I & II.

[8] Mark Granovetter, "The Strength of Weak Ties," *American Journal of Sociology* (May 1973) 78(6): 1360–80.

Trust was hard to come by. Connecting with strangers meant dealing with social differences, and working with limited knowledge of others. This resulted in ambiguous interactions, and anxiety about relations that could have corrosive effects. Sure knowledge of neighbors (even if hateful) was replaced by hazy conceptions of strangers—imaginings that could become nightmares. Dreams of amassing fortunes could turn into fears of being defrauded, leading to mistrust, intolerance, and demonizing of others. So, modern communities were built tenuously and produced hatred, stereotypes, and violence as well as practices of sharing.

PRINT INFRASTRUCTURE AND THE WARS OF RELIGION

Printing was the primary infrastructure that made the Reformation possible, and fueled the Wars of Religion. Printed Bibles and the spread of literacy allowed experiments in new forms of Christian practice that distinguished Protestants from Catholics. Reading God's word directly from a printed text was a transforming experience for members of Reformed faiths, and allowed individuals to dream differently about being good Christians. At the same time, printing amplified the rifts between faiths, engendering violence. Invidious distinctions were made not only between Catholics and Protestants, but also among Reformed groups that accused each other of being wolves in sheep's clothing (or false prophets).[9]

Printing could be so transforming in Reformation Europe because inexpensive Bibles exposed the foundations of the Christian faith. The Catholic Church had based its authority on exclusive knowledge of God's will and control of the written word. The scriptures were reproduced in monasteries and books were collected in monastic libraries. The clergy limited who could read and how people could interpret the Bible. Ideas about God other than those espoused by the Church were heresy and those who promoted those ideas would be killed—except where Moors and Jews were allowed their beliefs within their own communities. Christian thought—the dominant faith—was managed by the Catholic Church until the Reformation.[10]

With inexpensive Bibles available, Reformers could advocate independent study of the scriptures, teaching those with little social power how to read and think independently about God's will.[11] Revolutionary sentiments reverberated quickly across Europe as debates about Christianity disrupted traditions of power, too. The Church had defined nobles as closer to God than their social inferiors, but this was not part of the Bible. Peasants reading the scriptures on their own saw that God favored the weak even if the

---

[9] Elizabeth Eisenstein, *The Printing Press as an Agent of Change: Communication and Cultural Transformation in Early Modern Europe* (Cambridge: Cambridge University Press, 1979).

[10] Eisenstein, *The Printing Press as an Agent of Change*, vol. I; Jack Goody, *The Logic of Writing and the Organization of Society* (Cambridge: Cambridge University Press, 1986); Manguel, *A History of Reading*.

[11] Eisenstein, *The Printing Press as an Agent of Change*, vol. II; Ginzburg, *The Cheese and the Worms*.

Church favored those with power. So, members of Reformed faiths found good reason to become more modern and take responsibility for their own religious education.[12]

Michael Walzer[13] has described the Reformation as the first mass movement because it gave common purpose and practices to strangers who lived thousands of miles from one another. Religious propaganda defined communities and drew boundaries between sects. Belonging to a religion had never been just a matter of faith, but of communities of the faithful. Now communities of believers were imagined communities that included strangers from all across Europe.

The Counter-Reformation was the Catholic Church's response to its critics. Ridiculed by Martin Luther and others for lack of adherence to God's word, the Church made reforms, centralizing authority more securely in Rome, codifying doctrine, and purifying the faith of popular variants. The Counter-Reformation rejected the flexibility of practices that had characterized Catholicism, creating a very different moral landscape.[14]

As Peter Burke has argued, the reforms on both sides changed Christian practices, and weakened the cultural glue of popular traditions that had held towns together with religious festivities.[15] In some areas, traditions were maintained and expanded, but in many parts of Europe, communities imploded in violence as members of different faiths became warring factions.

Religious propaganda proliferated to justify the violence and spread the faith. Reformers portrayed the Church as incapable of protecting its flock, treating Catholicism as the problem rather than the solution to their woes (see Figure 2.1).

With the turn to propaganda, print became an infrastructure for developing modern intolerance: impersonal contempt for an institution. It was not only used to print vernacular Bibles, but also to create visual propaganda that debased the Pope. Martin Luther in his *New Testament* (1522) used sets of prints to compare the virtue of Jesus to the corruption of the Pope. With pictures of the Pope as morally unfit for teaching God's word and the Church as riddled with corruption, he helped engender disgust with Catholicism for betraying Christian values (see Figures 2.2 and 2.3).

The Wars of Religion were as bloody as they were morally fierce. Catholics and Protestants alike tried to take control of territories and towns by force, hoping to make their religion the only legitimate basis for community, but this only led to prolonged violence. The Wars of Religion drove people from their homes, fleeing into new areas to escape persecution. In places like Geneva and the Massachusetts Bay Colony, Reformers effectively set up strong communities of the faithful, but in most other areas, people were caught in battles over belief that never could be resolved by fighting.

---

[12] Eisenstein, *The Printing Press as an Agent of Change*, vol. II.

[13] Michael Walzer, *Revolution of the Saints* (Cambridge: Harvard University Press, 1965).

[14] Burke, *Popular Culture in Early Modern Europe*, chapter 8.

[15] Burke, *Popular Culture in Early Modern Europe*, chapter 8.

Johannis.

FIGURE 2.1 *Religious Propaganda Against the Catholic Church. Lucas Cranach,* Pope as Whore of Babylon, *1521*

The Wars of Religion were ended by establishing the principle of state sovereignty. It was a way of reconnecting people to places, and building communities of strangers within states. Sovereigns could set their own religious policies, according to the Augsburg Settlement of 1555. And sovereign states were protected from invasion for their policies

Paſſional Chꝛiſti vnd

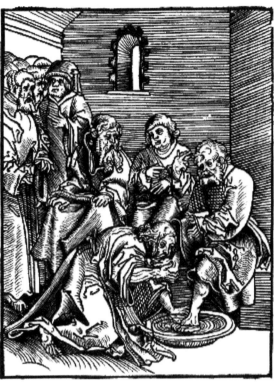

Chꝛiſtus.

Szo ich ewre fueſʒe habe gewaſchen d ich ewir herr vñ meyſter bin/vill meh: ſolt yr einander vnter euch die fuſʒe waſchen. Hie mit habe ich euch ein anʒeygung vñ beyſpiel geben/ wie ich ym than habe/ alſʒo ſolt yr hinfur auch thuen. Warlich warlich ſage ich euch/d knecht iſt nicht meh: dan ſeyn herre/ ſʒo iſt auch nicht d geſchickte botte meh: bñ d yn geſanbe hat/Wiſt yr das/ Selig ſeyt yr ſʒo yr das thuen werdent. Johan·13·

Antichꝛiſti.

Antichꝛiſtus.

Der Babſt maſt ſich an iʒlichen Tyrannen vnd heydniſchen furſten; ſʒo yre fueſʒ den leuten ʒu kuſſen dar gereicht/ nach ʒu volgen/damit es waer werde das geſchꝛieben iſt.Wilcher dieſer beſtien bild e nicht anbettet/ſall getöd werden. Apocalip·13· Diʒ kuſſens darff ſich der Babſt yn ſeynē decretalen vnwoꝛ ſchēbt rümen.c.cū oli dē pꝛi.cle.Si ſūmus pon.dē ſen.excś.

by the Peace of Westphalia in 1648, which allocated states defined territories that their sovereigns had the right to control. Those of a different faith were supposed to migrate to where they were welcome.[16]

This legitimated the development of states as communities of strangers. In states with one religion, people with the same belief were expected to accept refugees from

FIGURE 2.2 *Lucas Cranach,* Portrait of Christ and Anti-Christ. Feet Kissing, *1521*

---

[16] Stephen Krasner, *Sovereignty* (Princeton, NJ: Princeton University Press, 1999).

Paſſional Chꝛiſti vnd

Chꝛiſtus.

Die ſoldner haben geflochten eyne kronen von dôrnen / vñ auff
ſein heußt gedꝛuckt/ darnach mit eynem purper kleydt haben ſie
yn bekleydet.　　　　　　　Johan . 19.

Antichꝛiſt.

Antichꝛiſt .

Der Keyſer Conſtantinus hat vns die keyſerlich krone/geʒirde
aller andern geſchmuck in maſſen wie yhn ð keyſer tregt / purper cleyt alle andere cleyder vñ ſcepter ʒutragen vñ ʒubꝛauchen
geben c.Conſtantinus.cꝛvi.diſ. Solche lúgen haben ſie yre ty-
ranney ʒu erhalten ertich wyder alle hiſtorien vñ kuntſchaffe/
dan es iſt nit bꝛauchlich geweßen den Romiſchen Keyſern ein
ſolche krone ʒutragen.　　　　　　　A iij

FIGURE 2.3 *Lucas
Cranach*, Portrait of
Christ and Anti-Christ.
Christ Mocked, Pope
Venerated, *1521*

somewhere else. And states with policies of religious tolerance required members of different communities of faith to learn to live together.

THE PARISIAN WATER SUPPLY

The Wars of Religion were particularly intense and destructive in France, making peaceful coexistence a new dream of community. French Calvinists (Huguenots) were numerous and powerful in France, but the state was Catholic. Conflicts over who would dominate the country were ongoing and complex. The Edict of Nantes provided a legal framework for religious tolerance, but it was flagrantly violated in Paris during the St. Bartholomew's Day massacre (1572) when Huguenots were slaughtered in large numbers (see Figure 2.4).

Because of the religious violence, Paris became an untenable place to live and work—particularly for Huguenots. Artisans fled, depopulating the city and devastating its economy. So, when Henri IV ascended the throne in 1589, espousing tolerance and facing fierce Catholic opposition, he focused on making Paris a better city in which to live and work. He could not change anyone's religious convictions, but he could repair the city's infrastructure to uplift the community as a whole.[17]

Building an adequate water supply for Paris was at the heart of the effort to restore and repopulate the city. It was a way of luring artisans back, making the city more habitable, and stimulating the economy. Paris had a serious water supply problem. The right bank had only a few springs, and the left bank had no natural sources. So, Parisians were dependent on water sellers who carried fresh water through the streets in buckets.[18] The proposed water supply consisted of two major engineering enterprises: the Samaritaine Pump and the Rungis Aqueduc, often called the Aqueduc d'Arcueil. The pump was to raise water from the Seine River to supply the right bank. The aqueduct was to carry water from springs outside the city to the left bank.

FIGURE 2.4 *The Bartholomew Day Massacre. Dubois,* Le Massacre de la Saint-Barthélemy, c. *1572–84*

---

[17] Christopher Henke, "The Mechanics of Workplace Order: Toward a Sociology of Repair," *Berkeley Journal of Sociology* (2000), 44(4): 55–81.

[18] John Lough, *France Observed in the Seventeenth Century by British Travelers* (Boston: Oriel Press, 1985) 53–4.

FIGURE 2.5 *Plan of Paris in 1572*

Even before the Wars of Religion, lack of water had undermined the quality of life in Paris, limiting economic development and affecting sanitation. Since there was no water for irrigating gardens or cleaning streets, Paris became famous for its slippery muck and terrible smell. Not only families, but workplaces suffered. Making and dying textiles required water. So did tile making, printing, furniture making, and metallurgy. So, industries developed in Paris mainly by the river or the right bank's springs, limiting the geography of economic growth.[19]

The right bank—because it had more water—was much more populous than the left (see Figure 2.5). (Note that the left bank is on the right of the map and the right bank is on the left.)

---

[19] Karen Newman, *Cultural Capitals: Early Modern London and Paris* (Princeton, NJ: Princeton University Press, 2007), pp. 77–84.

The inhabited part of the left bank (right side of Figure 2.5) was much smaller than its counterpart on the other side. Even the market gardens beyond the city walls had developed only in limited regions where there was water. There was some tile making along the river and even cattle grazing on some of its islands because this is where there was water. But the muddy banks provided an unhealthy source of water for human consumption.

Repairing the city by improving the water supply was a way to demonstrate good stewardship, and important to politics after the Wars of Religion. Members of all Christian faiths agreed that Creation, or the earth itself, was a gift from God meant to support human life. Building infrastructure was a way to use this gift wisely, and put it to good purposes. Improving the Parisian water supply was a way for Henri IV to display moral leadership that was recognizable across faiths.[20]

Henri IV needed to demonstrate his moral leadership because his legitimacy as monarch of France was in question. He had been raised as a Huguenot by his mother, and he openly advocated religious tolerance—a stance that horrified France's Catholic elite. So, members of the Catholic League, questioning his moral standing to rule, stood ready to prevent him from entering Paris as France's new monarch. He placated them by converting to Catholicism, but they still did not trust him. So, he used stewardship practices to assert his legitimacy.[21]

The principles of stewardship that guided Henri IV were articulated by Olivier de Serres.[22] Serres wrote that states ought to be governed like estates, using knowledge of nature to use the land well. It was the moral duty of a king to make the land under his control more like the Garden of Eden, using natural resources to serve his people as well as possible.[23] Serres emphasized the importance of infrastructure to virtuous land management. Without water and transport, land could not be made abundant and useful. This was particularly true for cities, where more people shared less land. But for Serres, there was no point to reviving the city without endowing it with gardens.[24] Paris should be a paradise enjoyed together by strangers.

The Parisian water system started with the construction of the Samaritaine Pump (see Figure 2.6). It was located on Pont Neuf, a main bridge over the Seine in the center of Paris.[25] The waterwheels of the Samaritaine were rotated by the river current, powering pumps that raised water from the fresh flow in the middle of the river to a reservoir high on the right bank. From there it was piped to the Louvre Palace and its gardens. The gardens made Paris more like Eden, and the fountains provided water to residents, too.[26]

---

[20] Chandra Mukerji, "Material Practices of Domination: Christian Humanism: The Built Environment, and Techniques of Western Power," *Theory and Society* (Feb. 2002), 31(1): 1–34.

[21] Mukerji, "Material Practices of Domination"; Newman, *Cultural Capitals*.

[22] Olivier de Serres, *Du Théâtre d'Agriculture et Mesnage des Champs* (Paris: I. Méyater, 1600).

[23] Mukerji, "Material Practices of Domination".

[24] Serres, *Du Théâtre d'Agriculture et Mesnage des Champs*.

[25] Edward Fournier, *Histoire du Pont-Neuf* (Paris: E. Dentu, 1862).

[26] Hillary Ballon, *The Paris of Henry IV: Architecture and Urbanism* (Cambridge: MIT Press, 1994); Fournier, 1862.

LA POMPE DE LA SAMARITAINE qui est derriere la seconde Arche du Pontneuf du côté du Louvre, fut bâtie sous Henri 3. pour conduire de l'eau dans un Reservoir qui paroit encore devant le Port de l'École ; mais ce Reservoir n'aiant point servi, l'eau de cette Pompe qui est aspirante et de l'invention du S.ʳ Ioly, a été conduite par des tuyaux au Chateau et Iardin des Thuileries, dont elle fait iouer les jets du Parterre. Les Figures de Nôtre Seigneur et de la Samaritaine sont des copies de celles que fit alors Germain Pilon fameux Sculpteur. Le Timbre de l'Horloge est accompagné d'un Carillon qui sonne aux heures, et qui a été refait en 168, que le Bâtiment a été assez renouvelé et augmenté de plusieurs ornemens, et d'un Cadran Anemonique, qui par le moien d'une Renommee tournante au gre du vent, se hausse quand l'air est pesant, et se baisse quand il est leger, et marque les vents sur des Cadrans.
A Paris chez I. Mariette rue S.ᵗ Iacques à la Victoire Avec Privilege du Roi

FIGURE 2.6

Samaritaine Pump on the Pont Neuf. Nicolas-Jean-Baptiste Raguenet, Le Point-Neur et la Pompe de la Samaritain vus du Quai de la Mégisserie, *1777*

The pump was named after the Good Samaritan in the Bible who, in spite of his own marginality, helped a Jew in trouble even though Jews were supposed to be his enemy. This story of reconciliation and care for one's enemies provided an apt symbol for Henri IV's water supply. The water system was a way of joining antagonistic groups with an infrastructure of tolerance.

Henri IV was assassinated before the water system expanded to the left bank. But Henri IV's widow, Marie de' Medici, ordered construction of the Rungis Aqueduct to the left bank. It carried water from sources outside the city to the Luxembourg Palace, its gardens, and a nearby hospital, la Charité. The left bank finally had its own water supply.[27]

---

[27] Fournier, *Histoire du Pont-Neuf*, pp. 179–84. Georg Simmel, "The Metropolis and Mental Life," in Gary Bridge and Sophie Willson (eds), *The Blackwell City Reader* (Oxford and Walden, MA: Wiley-Blackwell, [1903] 2002); Georg Simmel, *The Sociology of Georg Simmel* (Glencoe, IL: Free Press, 1950).

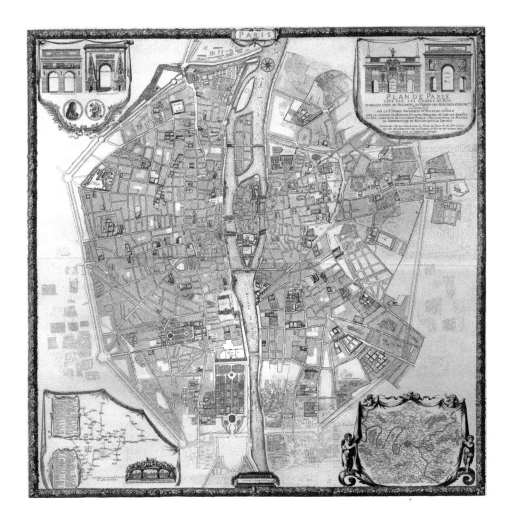

FIGURE 2.7 *Bullet &
Blondel 1676 Map of
Paris*

By the end of the 17th century, the Samaritaine Pump had tripled the supply to the
right bank, and the Rungis Aqueduct brought even more water to the left bank. Paris
was a very different place, in part because the water supply allowed it to develop in new
areas—particularly on the left bank. Dozens of neighborhood fountains were added to
the system, too—including famous ones at Saint Victor and the Porte Saint-Michel.

The results were notable. By 1676, development on the left bank (see the right side of
the Bullet and Blondel map of Paris in Figure 2.7) almost equaled that of the right bank.
And even the right bank had expanded beyond the old city walls, as some of the suburbs
were incorporated into the city.

Paris became a modern community of strangers sharing a common infrastructure,
held together by dreams of governmental stewardship. The water supply built by Henri

IV was limited, but this did not diminish the admiration from Parisians for his caring stewardship of their city. The city was joined with ties that did not bind—a water system and cultural imaginary of political stewardship. Parisians could make choices about where and how to live, and take their evening promenades together in gardens "restored" to a perfection reminiscent of Eden. They became entangled strangers who organized their lives around the same water, markets, bridges, and ways of life without making immediate demands on one another.

Paris became a social world in which citizens had a common identity based on where they lived and expectations of stewardship from government. But it was also a place where people pursued lives indifferent to each other, developing what Simmel[28] described as the blasé attitude of modern urban life. Paris was a community in which this indifference mattered, allowing modern individuals to be different from each other without sacrificing their identity as members of the same city.

[28] Georg Simmel, "The Metropolis and Mental Life," in Gary Bridge and Sophie Willson (eds), *The Blackwell City Reader* (Oxford and Walden, MA: Wiley-Blackwell, [1903] 2002).

CHAPTER THREE

Cultural Imaginaries
and Modern States

The power of cultural imaginaries to transform social relations was made vivid in 17th-century France. The state administration initiated a cultural experiment in the arts that helped to turn France into one of the strongest states in Europe. Jean-Baptiste Colbert, Louis XIV's minister of the Treasury and director of the king's household (1665–83), cultivated a political imaginary of France's classical heritage and imperial destiny that was at once challenging and seductive to nobles. The state in France had previously been weak because French nobles exercised considerable autonomy, but refusing an imperial destiny was hard for them. The administration had no way to win them over through patrimonial politics so it subordinated nobles to the king with a dream.

French nobles had vexed the reign of Henri IV, and they were prepared to limit the authority of the young Louis XIV, but this did not come to pass. After roughly twenty-five years on the throne, Louis XIV was ruling a system of state "absolutism". He was so powerful that many people characterized him as a tyrant. And French families of the highest ranks of the nobility established residency at Versailles, taking their place on the public stage the king had established and ruled. What happened?

In part, the modern states that developed in the 17th and 18th centuries—including France—were able to take advantage of the principles of state sovereignty laid out in the Treaty of Augsburg and Peace of Westphalia, gaining greater control of their territories and improving them with infrastructure. But this still left many nobles with important political offices over which they exercised independent powers. Political decisions required their consultation and assent, so noble officials continued to exercise personal rather than impersonal power.[1]

---

[1] Compare to Max Weber's conception of the modern state as a mode of impersonal rule. See Max Weber, Gunther Roth, and Claus Wittich, *Economy and Society: An Outline of Interpretive Sociology* (Berkeley: University of California Press, 1978), pp. 996–8.

The cultural program of classical revival made all the difference in France. It did not provoke confrontation between the king and nobility. Instead, it provided a dream of collective glory and modern political efficacy based on the achievements of the ancients in Gaul. (Gaul had been a major province of the Roman Empire.) Conjuring up this history for those who frequented the French court reminded nobles of how important France had been and how unimportant it had become. Under Charlemagne, France had unified and ruled the Holy Roman Empire. In the 17th century, France was just a small kingdom surrounded by enemies. Nobles had considerable autonomous powers in their regions, but what was that compared to ruling an empire? Not so much.

The ancient world could have been dismissed as a lost past, but Colbert did not allow it. He orchestrated a classical revival in the arts to claim Rome's imperial heritage for France, and make this idea seem plausible. Louis XIV became the Sun King, Apollo, who brought abundance to the earth with his warmth and light. He was a force of nature (see Figure 3.1) too strong to stop from realizing his destiny.[2]

The image of Louis XIV's imperial destiny was devised by scholars in Colbert's "petite académie". This group of advisors studied ancient texts and artifacts to find classical means for celebrating Louis XIV. They proposed projects to be realized by artists and artisans patronized by the state. Colbert also came to rely on Charles Le Brun, the head of the Académie royale de peinture et de sculpture, to design the immersive environment of classical revival at Versailles. In the king's gardens and residence, nobles walked among statues of ancient gods and heroes put there to further the administration's cultural program. They also played roles in performances in the gardens based on tales of the ancient world that were organized by members of the king's household.[3]

While French writers argued that the moderns could never match the ancients in culture, knowledge, and power, artisans and artists silently suggested the opposite with their work. Jacob Soll[4] has argued that Colbert gained power for the state by collecting ancient legal documents and using them to subordinate the Church to the king. But the king also had to subordinate the nobility, and Colbert made this possible with art and artifacts rather than legal papers. He cultivated noble taste for the glories of empire, and made the king seem capable of realizing imperial dreams. One could easily deny the idea

---

[2] This was not the only imaginary used in the formation of modern states. History and destiny were organized around other principles, too. See Julia Adams, *The Familial State* (Ithaca: Cornell University Press, 2005); George Steinmetz, *State/Culture: State-Formation after the Cultural Turn* (Ithaca, NY: Cornell University Press, 1999).

[3] Claire Goldstein, *Vaux and Versailles* (Philadelphia: University of Pennsylvania Press, 2008); Chandra Mukerji, "Space and Political Pedagogy at the Gardens of Versailles," *Public Culture* (2012), 24(3), 68: 509–34; Mukerji, *Territorial Ambitions*.

[4] Jacob Soll, *The Information Master: Jean-Baptiste Colbert's Secret State Intelligence System* (Ann Arbor: University of Michigan Press, 2009); William Beik, *Absolutism and Society in Seventeenth-Century France: State Power and Provincial Aristocracy in Languedoc* (Cambridge: Cambridge University Press, 1985).

FIGURE 3.1 *Apollo, the Sun King. Jean Bérain,* Apollo on his Chariot, *1680–1710*

that Louis XIV was a Sun King, but it was harder to deny his capacity to change the world around him. Machines in theatrical productions carried Apollo through the skies on his chariot, the fountains at Versailles sparkled in the sun, and the Hall of Mirrors in the chateau captured the sun's warmth and light in a dramatic display of ingenuity and wealth. Artisans made collective future glory conceivable, drawing members of the great families of France to the king's side to share his imperial ambitions.

The garden at Versailles was a masterpiece of territorial control, using techniques of military engineering and ancient garden design to make a beautifully managed landscape worthy of Rome. The chateau was filled with paintings and tapestries that represented the king as Apollo (see Figure 3.2), and was outfitted with furniture that glowed like the sun with metal and shell inlay. The statues in the garden were either imitations of Roman

FIGURE 3.2 *The Apollo Fountain, showing Apollo on his Chariot Bringing the Sun into the Sky. Photo by Becky Cohen*

ones or done in Roman style. This display of luxury and use of classical themes made Roman revival seem already in process, and beyond dispute. Versailles was an Olympus that nobles could inhabit.[5]

The elites from high noble families that were given residence in the chateau were immersed in and seduced by this cultural imaginary. They were not captured by the king as Norbert Elias[6] has suggested; they found themselves wanting the future he offered. Nobles at court participated in plays, acting out stories of ancient heroism in which they ascended to Mt. Olympus to join the gods. They helped to bring the ancient world to life, and experienced this way what an imperial future might bring.[7]

[5] Jean-Pierre Neraudau, *L'Olympe du Roi-Soleil: Mythologie et Ideologie Royale au Grand Siècle* (Paris: Les Belles Lettres, 1986).

[6] Norbert Elias, *The Court Society*, trans. Edmund Jephcott (Dublin: University of Dublin Press, 1969).

[7] Dorothy Holland, William S. Lachicotte, Jr., Debra Skinner, and Carole Cain, *Identity and Agency in Cultural Worlds* (Cambridge, MA: Harvard University, 1998).

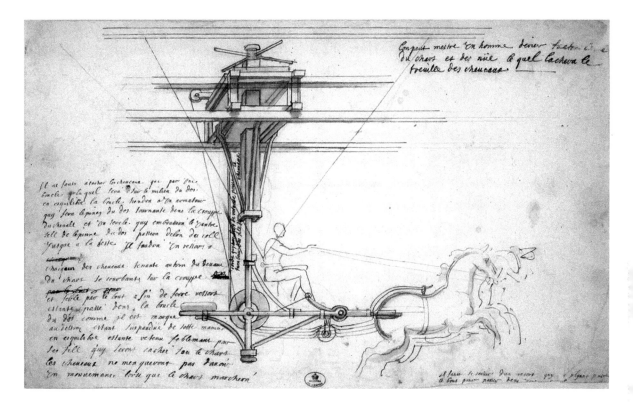

IMMERSIVE THEATER AND POLITICAL SPECTACLE

FIGURE 3.3 *Chariot of the Sun (on Pulleys). Jean Bérain, Menus Plaisirs, 1692–1702*

Noble immersion in the classical past was active rather than passive. Courtiers took on assigned roles in plays, ballets, and mock battles, reviving the ancient world through participatory spectacles. They put on costumes, learned choreography, and entered sets that pulled them around with pulley and ropes, all to conjure up the cultural imaginary of Louis XIV's Olympus.[8] These entertainments were meant to fill their idle hours, but they were also political games of seduction (see Figure 3.3).[9]

The festivities at Versailles were so frequent and elaborate that they gave the court a reputation for frivolousness. The spectacles seemed just games of make-believe, dressing up, and playing roles. The festivities were often announced as rewards for the nobles who were returning from wars fought for the king. Parties provided time to shed serious cares, play a fool, battle phantoms, and animate wild creatures. There were monsters to defeat

---

[8] Néraudau, *L'Olympe du Roi-Soleil*.

[9] Sherry Ortner, *Anthropology and Social Theory: Culture, Power, and the Acting Subject* (Durham and London: Duke University Press, 2006).

FIGURE 3.4 *Design of Special Effects for Spectacles: Roaring Monster. Menus Plaisirs*

outside of war, and virtues to uphold in mock battles. The spectacles were made magical as well as entertaining with highly engineered special effects, too, using ingenuity to animate make-believe classical worlds (see Figure 3.4).[10]

The events were carnivalesque, borrowing the term from Mikhail Bakhtin.[11] Bringing the past alive in the present seemed a cultural reversal of sorts—much like Carnival. During Carnival, people abandoned their normal character, dressed in costumes, and participated in games and parades that made fun of virtue and celebrated vice (see Figure 3.5). Peasants were crowned kings and queens, and ruled over a land of inversions. Overindulgence in sex and food was condoned, and piety set aside as people enacted roles outside normal conventions.[12] Dressing up and acting in plays and ballets at Versailles provided carnivalesque relief from the burdens of power, and seemed a time for machines and monsters to rule—only to be defeated.

Carnivalesque entertainments like masquerades were staples of court life, making light of games of power and the airs of the powerful. Costumes could be demeaning of

[10] Chandra Mukerji, *Territorial Ambitions and the Gardens of Versailles* (Cambridge: Cambridge University Press, 1997).

[11] Mikhail Bakhtin, *Rabelais and His World* (Bloomington: Indiana University Press, 1984).

[12] Peter Burke, *Popular Culture in Early Modern Europe* (London: Temple Smith, 1978).

FIGURE 3.5 *The World Turned Upside Down in Carnival. Pieter Bruegel the Elder,* The Fight between Carnival and Lent, *1559*

those who wore them—like the jester and snail costumes in Figures 3.6 and 3.7. The cultural conventions of patrimonial authority had to be dropped to play these roles, and nobles had a chance to laugh at themselves and their pretenses.

It seemed innocent on the surface, but playing out stories from classical mythology was a serious game of power and politics. Those who overacted a part one day could find themselves later dreaming of glory, heroically triumphing over France's enemies. In a world of noble modernity, dressing up could become a moment self-fashioning and an embrace of a new political ambition.

Where carnivalesque play was blurred with the imperial imagery, patrimonial relations were set aside—replaced by classical glory (Figure 3.8). In the frivolity, nobles were exposed to new ways of imagining themselves, subject to serious games of political seduction.

LEARNING BY DOING

The courtiers who were given roles in plays and ballets at Versailles had to try to make stories of the ancients come alive. They did not have to believe that Louis XIV was really a Sun King; they only had to make the power of Apollo and the rule of Olympus seem

FIGURE 3.6 *Costume for a Jester. Workshop of Jean Bérain, n.d.*

FIGURE 3.7 *Costume for a Snail. Menus Plaisirs*

FIGURE 3.8 *Conjuring Up Gods. Jean Bérain,* Neptune, *1680–1710*

convincing on stage (see Figure 3.9). Their bodies were drawn into realities that their minds might have refused, using their bodies as they were directed to do. Participants could laugh at the game and enjoy the spectacle, but they were still immersed in a political imaginary they had to try to animate. They could not struggle for autonomy in these roles, but they could feel imperial desires. The Olympus at Versailles was a giddy height to reach and an enticing reality to enter (see Figure 3.10).[13]

The playful activities at Versailles seem orthogonal to the serious business of governing. But the imperial scenarios showed what a strong state could do by coordinating powers of heaven and earth. As Huizinga argued in *Homo Ludens*,[14] by teaching people rules of play, games give players skills in using those rules. So, playing with imperial power and practicing how to revive Rome taught nobles forms of play that supported new logics of political action.

---

[13] Holland et al., *Identity and Agency*; Mukerji, "Space and Political Pedagogy"; Néraudeau, *L'Olympe du Roi-Soleil*.

[14] Johan Huizinga, *Homo Ludens: A Study of the Play Element in Culture* (London: Routledge & Kegan Paul, 1955).

FIGURE 3.9 *Set Design for the Domain of the Gods. Jean Bérain,* Le Mariage de Pluton et de Proserpine, *1680*

THE POWER OF THE ARTISANS

This cultural program was orchestrated at the Louvre in Paris. Louis XIV had insisted on making Versailles his residence, leaving the royal palace in Paris almost empty. In order to keep the Louvre inhabited and useful to the administration, Colbert turned the palace into an administrative center and workshop for crafting the dream world of Rome.

Originally, Colbert asked the royal architect, Louis Le Vau, to design a wing to connect the Louvre along the river to the Tuileries Palace, hoping this would make Paris more attractive to the king. Le Vau designed a well-appointed theater, and large and elegant new galleries that nobles could use for passage between the palaces or for holding parties. Beneath the galleries, the architect designed workshops and residences for artisans working on projects for the king's household. Louis XIV still refused to live in Paris, so the minister used the Louvre to house artists and artisans and provide rooms for some of the royal academies, creating a center for realizing his cultural program.[15]

---

[15] Jean-Claude Daufresne, *Louvre & Tuileries: Architectures de Papier* (Bruxelles: Pierre Mardaga, 1987), chapter 3.

FIGURE 3.10 *Heavenly Powers and Heavenly Beings. Jean Bérain,* Gloire de Venus, *1680–1703*

Artisans came from many parts of France to serve the king and work at the Louvre: sculptors, cabinetry makers, clock makers, instrument makers, a watch maker, painters, lens makers, a gun designer, and stage engineers. They decorated the royal households and gardens, and made luxury goods for nobles, too. They made clockworks for scientific study, and then used the same type of clockwork for decorative timepieces. They designed decorations for ships in the Royal Navy, and engineered stages and special effects for the spectacles at Versailles. They made, in other words, the cultural imaginary of the Sun King and the world of French classical revival.[16]

The Académie Française, the Academy of Painting and Sculpture, and Colbert's "petite académie" or Academy of Inscriptions and Belles-Lettres were the three academies allocated space in the Louvre. While the Académie Française was defining and protecting French language and culture, the Academy of Inscriptions and Belle-Lettres was designing the overall program of classical revival for Colbert. And the Academy of

---

[16] Pierre Ramond, *André-Charles Boulle, Ébéniste, Ciseleur & Marqueteur Ordinaire du Roy* (Dourdan: Vial, 2011), pp. 42–5.

Painting and Sculpture, directed by Charles Le Brun, determined the aesthetic criteria and visual themes for the cultural program. Le Brun was also in charge of the interior decoration at Versailles, helped design garden statuary there, and directed the royal manufacture, or Gobelins factory that supplied furnishings, showing artists and artisans how to achieve the cultural goals of the program.[17]

The academies and workshops in tandem made the Louvre a kind of administrative center for the arts—full of scholars, artists, and artisans. They provided the principles of practice for luring nobles into imperial desire. These architects of the administration's political program were not nobles themselves, and were in service to the king. But they exercised enormous power over the high nobility at court by shaping the political imaginaries that their social superiors would learn.

The entertainments at court were mainly organized by Menus Plaisirs du Roi (the small pleasures of the king), an office of the king's household that included some of the artisans housed at the Louvre. The Menus Plaisirs was composed of a cadre of event planners, set designers, stage engineers, costume designers, furniture makers, and artisans. They did many things to entertain the royal family and court. They hired comedians, fashioned jewelry for the royal family and distinguished guests, made toys and furniture for the royal children, and created gifts for visitors to Versailles. But their most important function was to design the major events and parties at Versailles—the spectacles that defined the theater of power.[18]

The Menus Plaisirs was directed by Jean Bérain, a gifted designer who worked in many media. He drew most of the costumes for dances and parties, designed sets and special effects for plays and ballets, and staged the fêtes and divertissements at Versailles in the royal garden. He also was given space at the Louvre.

Members of the Menus Plaisirs dressed up nobles and designed stages where they could act out scenarios of power. They designed the chariots to carry Apollo or other gods on pulleys through the sky, designed monsters that could wiggle and roar, and burned down sets with fireworks (see Figures 3.11 and 3.12). Their staging, costumes, and special effects gave the heroes in court entertainments extraordinary powers, and conjured up forces evil enough to make their battles worthy of great men.

Nobles may have played powerful figures in the dramas, but they were not in control of the stories or their own actions on stage. They were caught in costumes and on sets that defined how they should behave.

---

[17] Goldstein, *Vaux and Versailles*; Mukerji, *Territorial Ambitions*.

[18] Jérôme de La Gorce, *Dans l'Atelier des Menus Plaisirs du Roi. Spectacles, Fêtes et Cérémonies aux XVIIe et XVIIIe Siècles* (Paris: Archives Nationales-Versailles, Artlys, 2010); Antoine Levesque, *Receuil de Decorations de Theatre par Monsieur Levesque, Garde General des Magasins des Menus Plaisirs de la Chambre* (Paris: Archives Nationales, 1752), CP/O/1/3238.

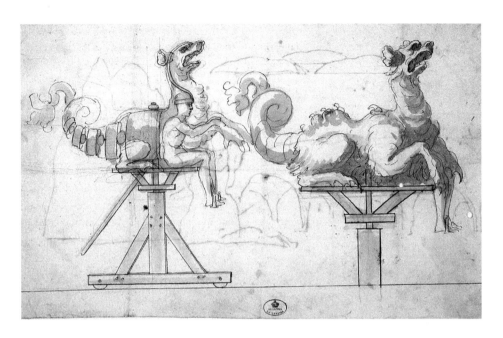

FIGURE 3.11 *Theatrical Engineering and Performance of Monsters. Jean Bérain,* Man Animating a Monster for Bellérophon, *1679*

FIGURE 3.12 *Trap Doors and Elevators for the Stage. Jean Bérain,* A Trap for Staging the Metamorphosis, *n.d.*

FIGURE 3.13 *The Triumph of the Sun King. Jean Bérain,* Apollo on his Celestial Chariot, *1700–5*

As we have seen,[19] clothing in the Renaissance was a tool of personal moral formation. Dress was used to demonstrate patterns of mutual obligation, and fashion emotional as well as functional ties. So, when nobles put on costumes to play roles in dramas, it was both a game and a moment of moral fashioning that required them to think about their ability to act as gods and heroes in stories of classical grandeur. Taking on such a role was to shoulder moral responsibilities, and to become adequate to the demands of the role assigned them.

Enough nobles were seduced by the dream world of the Sun King that they placed hope in the king's imperial ambitions (see Figure 3.13). They still emphasized their autonomy, but they ceded power to the state to realize their dreams of empire.

THE MODERN STATE

Peter Burke[20] has argued that the propaganda promoting Louis XIV as the Sun King, including the art program, theater, and artifacts, failed miserably because in other countries people laughed at the pretensions of the French king. Written propaganda about the glorious life at Versailles was easy to ridicule, and equating Louis XIV with Apollo was easy to reject as absurd. But Louis XIV's main political problem was not to raise his international standing, but to reduce the autonomy of French nobles that had hindered previous French kings. The administration's cultural policy did this effectively. When nobles entered into heavenly firmaments, subordinating themselves to the Sun King, Apollo, they relinquished themselves at least in part to the machinery of power.

The surprise was how quickly this cultural program worked to transfer powers to the state. Twenty-five years after Louis XIV took the throne, the administration had radically altered relations of power. The art and architecture of classical revival had successfully entangled dreams and reality in new ways. Transferring powers to the state had been convincingly portrayed as a way to seek greater grandeur, take hold of history, and speak collectively to posterity about the French heritage. So, nobles put on their costumes, and the king became ruler of a modern state. Forms of agency that had belonged only to individuals now were coordinated to fulfill dreams of history and destiny through the exercise of institutional power.

---

[19] Ann Rosalind Jones and Peter Stallybrass, *Renaissance Clothing and the Materials of Memory* (Cambridge: Cambridge University Press, 2000).

[20] Peter Burke, *The Fabrication of Louis XIV* (Bath: The Bath Press, 1994).

CHAPTER FOUR

DISCURSIVE MODERNITY AND GLOBAL INDUSTRIAL CAPITALISM

Modernity started to change in the 17th and 18th centuries as major thinkers began to articulate and promote principles of modern culture. Modern selves, communities, and states had been developing until this point around dreams of possibility rather than principles. So, developing criteria for distinguishing what was modern from what was not and for measuring progress was a shift of profound importance. It reoriented modern life away from shared cultural imaginaries and toward impersonal standards. Progress began to be equated with the pursuit of private property and industrial production, too, so efforts to modernize fueled the development of capitalism and the industrial production of modern things. Principles of modernity became self-reinforcing as spaces from factories, cities, hotels, and stores to libraries and homes came to embody conceptions of modern progress (see Figure 4.1). Discursive modernity became hard to escape or think beyond.[1]

Modern life had been from its inception destructive, ambitious, and transforming, but discursive modernity was conceptually standardized and more physically encompassing. It seemed to close around people, devouring the landscape, limiting what was possible to do, and colonizing categories of thought. It was giddy to span ever wider rivers with bridges, and link ports around the world with steam ships, but it was terrifying, too, to see factories dominate the horizon and pollute rivers, and to justify the poverty of cities and slavery in colonies as key to progress. There were fortunes to be made, but lives were being ruined and human agency undermined.[2]

---

[1] Henri Lefebvre, *The Production of Space* (Oxford and Cambridge, MA: Blackwell, 1991); David Harvey, *Spaces of Capital: Towards a Critical Geography* (New York: Routledge, 2001). The global pattern of trade is described by Immanuel Wallerstein in *The Modern World-System* (New York: Academic Press, 1974).

[2] Karl Marx and Friedrich Engels, *Capital* (New York: International Publishers, 1967).

Figure 4.1 *Factories Surrounding Manchester, England.* William Wyld, Manchester from Kersal Moor, *Wikimedia, 1852*

It was not meant to be this way. The philosophers who set down modern principles over the long 18th century had utopian ambitions: seeking knowledge of human nature and human relationships to nature to rationalize social and material life for the benefit of all (see Figure 4.2). Their starting point was a scientific turn in political philosophy to ground prescriptions in reality. The purpose was to construct a conceptual apparatus for improving politics and making more progressive societies and economies. Principles of modern existence were supposed to be derived from what was natural for humans to do and want from life. Modern individuals were still responsible for their lives, but now there were standards of progress and rationality to guide them.

As Bauman[3] has argued, the articulation of modern principles gave a destructive power to modernity. The criteria of adequacy spelled out this way added to the anxiety of everyday existence by posing the question of who did or did not meet standards. Progress toward modernity was a measure of individuals, cities, and states, assessing their levels of rationality and civilization. Groups now had to aspire to what was defined as naturally human.

Modern social forms of the self, community, and state had been mute, material experiments in the 14th to 18th centuries. They had been silently conjured up around dreams of possibility with inarticulate things: clothes, infrastructure, and art. What was truly modern was not distinguished from what was not. People used old terms like natural nobility

---

[3] Zygmunt Bauman, *Modernity and Ambivalence* (London: Polity Press, 1993), chapters 1 and 2.

FIGURE 4.2 *Newton as Geometer, the Icon of Scientific Rationality. William Blake,* Newton. *c. 1795*

to describe fashionable elites without noble rank. Modern communities were described in terms of stewardship, and modern states were associated with extant understandings of classical revival. Old terms made modern social forms and types seem continuous with the past.

In contrast, the Enlightenment vocabulary for characterizing modernity was designed to create a decisive break with the past, making the modern something to recognize, seek, and desire. The modern world was now elevated to the pinnacle of civilization and human achievement because it was founded on rational principles and used scientific knowledge for material advancement (see Figure 4.3).

Individuals who had previously dreamed about and improvised what to do next now faced scripts for proper action, standards of competence, and measures of success. Personal accountability had been transformed into practices of accounting. Articulating modern principles did not make Europeans modern, as Bruno Latour[4] has argued. But modern discourses were used to produce what Foucault[5] called a new order of things.

---

[4]Bruno Latour, *We Have Never Been Modern* (Cambridge: Harvard University Press, 1993).
[5]Michel Foucault, *The Order of Things; An Archeology of the Human Sciences* (New York: Penguin Books, 1971).

FIGURE 4.3 *Exposition of Civilization. J. McNeven,* The Interior of the Crystal Palace in London during the Great Exhibition of 1851

PHILOSOPHICAL MODERNITIES

Modern discourse in the 18th century focused on forms of modernity that already existed, finding words for debating their proper design and significance. Thomas Hobbes[6] asserted the importance of strong states, John Locke[7] extolled the virtue of (weak) contractual relationships, and Jean-Jacques Rousseau[8] described how to make modern selves good citizens. They debated how to engineer selves, communities, and states rather than tinkering with possibilities, taking advantage of human rationality to structure new conditions of well-being.

Thomas Hobbes[9] defined the modern by its opposite: a primitive state of nature. Civilization was a shift from social relations based on irrational (primitive) impulses to those based on rational (modern) understandings of self-interest. People, he claimed,

---

[6] Thomas Hobbes, *Leviathan*, ed. C. MacPherson (London: Penguin Classics, 1982).

[7] John Locke, *The John Locke Collection: 6 Classic Works* (Waxkeep Publishing, 2013), Kindle edition.

[8] Jean-Jacques Rousseau, *Émile* (Heritage Illustrated Publishing, 2014), Kindle edition; Peter Alexander Meyers, *Abandoned to Ourselves* (New Haven: Yale, 2013).

[9] Hobbes, *Leviathan*.

wanted to impose their will and beliefs on others, and this naturally created a war of all against all. This is why, he contended, people needed to agree to be governed for their own good, accepting a social contract. For a government capable of enforcing the contract, he advocated a strong state—a commonwealth—that could provide the kind of structure individuals needed to reason and flourish.[10]

John Locke[11] thought the key to modernity lay in communities loosely integrated with contractual relations—not in strong states. The contract, for Locke, was by definition limited, consensual, and egalitarian, and thus in principle, the ideal bond for modern relations. He argued that people were naturally selfish, but not willfully domineering, so while they needed a social contract, they did not need a tyrannical state. The point of government was to check selfishness without foregoing freedom, and this, Locke argued, was best achieved through democracy and the separation of Church and state.[12] Locke rejected state stewardship as a form of paternalism that forged relations of dependence, but he nonetheless believed that governments needed to protect the natural rights of individuals.

Locke articulated liberal ideas about property, too. People should benefit from their labor, he argued. So, individuals had a right to the lands they improved and commodities they made. Giving individuals contractual rights to property was an incentive to progress.[13] But Locke limited the allocation of "natural" rights only to self-governing subjects who measured up to his principles of capability and rationality. To manage those he deemed unfit to govern themselves, Locke wrote the constitution for the Carolinas, including rules of slavery, and he spent part of his life working for the East India Company, advocating colonial subjugation of people in India.[14]

Jean-Jacques Rousseau[15] saw modernity starting not with states or contractual relations, but rather with individuals. So, he outlined principles of education for raising good citizens. People had to learn to use their freedom rationally, and understand their dependence on others, so they would recognize that the social contract was necessary to their happiness. Rousseau thought human weakness rather than greed or violence made life unhappy. He argued that the Creator had left a perfect world in human hands, and humans had corrupted it. His solution was to make people mentally and morally strong enough through education so they could achieve their own happiness and not become

---

[10] Hobbes, *Leviathan*, Part II.

[11] Locke, *The John Locke Collection*.

[12] John Locke, "A Letter Concerning Toleration," *The John Locke Collection*, pp. 16–41.

[13] John Locke, "Of Property," "Two Treatises on Government Book II: Of Civil Government," *The John Locke Collection*, p. 115.

[14] John Locke, "The Fundamental Constitution of Carolina," pp. 2–16; and "On Slavery," "Two Treatises on Government, Book II: Of Civil Government," *The John Locke Collection*, p. 114.

[15] Jean-Jacques Rousseau, *Émile* (Heritage Illustrated Publishing, 2014) Kindle edition; Peter Alexander Meyers, *Abandoned to Ourselves* (New Haven: Yale, 2013), Parts I and II.

corrupt. Truly rational citizens would make a better society because they would know how to balance the desire for freedom with the need for accommodating others. He added, however, that women would not benefit from such an education and could never have the full rationality of a citizen.[16]

These and other writers replaced the vague cultural imaginaries of modern possibility with precise definitions of progress or civilization. They advocated accountability in government, contracts, and citizens, and made material accomplishment the standard measure of progress. They called for free thought and free speech to make modern progress a matter of debate, but they also gave modernity articulated limits. Modern life was still supposed to be improvised by self-fashioning individuals, but now there were rules of good citizenship, contractual relations, and progress to which modern selves were accountable. And those people or groups who did not meet the criteria of modernity could now legitimately be deprived of rights.

Since capitalist manufacture and trade were defined as rational forms of economic life, industrialization became the emblem as well as the tool of modern progress. The British cotton industry provided a model of how to mass-produce goods to address the needs of modern individuals. Entrepreneurs learned to mass-produce inexpensive printed cottons that ordinary people could afford to use to imitate fashionable dress. The colorful cottons imitated and replaced Indian calicoes already in use as cheap replacements for embroideries. British industrialists took advantage of the calico craze, and got rich producing pretty cottons at a low price.[17]

As industry grew, cities grew rapidly and chaotically as peasants streamed into cities for work. The common lands on which many peasants had depended for survival started to be enclosed and claimed as private property as capitalist conceptions of ownership spread. Unable to support themselves, people from the countryside migrated to look for jobs in factories. At the same time, colonists established plantations and grew cotton with slave labor to sell to factories in Britain. Vast tracts of land in the Americas and elsewhere were used for cotton fields, and both Africans and Native Americans were taken as slaves and forced to work in cotton fields (see Figure 4.4). In pursuit of modern progress, land, plants, and people were reduced to industrial resources.

The cotton industry was not the only new manufacture in Britain; iron began to be mass-produced, too, with equally lucrative and destructive results. In England and Wales, coal and ore were dug from the earth to make iron for steam engines or to use in factories or on ships. Near mines, valleys were filled with slag. Woodlands were lumbered to build housing, and coal was used to make steam, producing smog. Steam ships, railroads, roads, factories, warehouses, and new ports moved the industrial commodities through a global

---

[16] Meyers, *Abandoned to Ourselves*, Parts I and II.

[17] Chandra Mukerji, *From Graven Images: Patterns of Modern Materialism* (New York: Columbia University Press, 1983), chapters 5 and 6.

network through which flowed liberal values and scientific ideas, too.[18] By the accounting principles of Locke's modernity, this was progress.

FIGURE 4.4 *Slave Labor in Oklahoma Cotton Field*

MODERN NATION STATES

Modern states flourished by turning modern principles into material practices for acting in history and realizing destinies. They also became nation-states as they developed common ways of life and distinctive collective commitments to modern principles. Each gained a distinct identity, with its own approach to modernity crafted to fit its citizens and its sense of destiny. States built infrastructures to create communities of strangers, rationalized bureaucracies to depersonalize power, and developed modern arsenals and armies to compete against other states. With their distinctive ways of pursuing modern futures, each state claimed a path forward as a leader of modernity.

---

[18] Harold Cook, *Matters of Exchange: Commerce, Medicine, and Science in the Dutch Golden Age* (New Haven: Yale University Press, 2007); Kapil Raj, *Relocating Modern Science: Circulation and the Construction of Knowledge in South Asia and Europe, 1650–1900* (New York: Palgrave Macmillan, 2007); Paul Mantoux, *The Industrial Revolution in the Eighteenth Century* (London: Jonathan Cape, revised edition, 1961).

Some states modernized by adopting forms of enlightened despotism. Following Hobbes, both Frederick the Great in Prussia and Catherine the Great in Russia built strong states, using bureaucratic reforms to reduce the power of the nobility in government and gain better control of the military by the state. Frederick expanded Prussian territory using the army and established new settlements that reclaimed land by rational means. Catherine the Great emphasized education and the arts, too, Westernizing Russian culture. Both corresponded with Voltaire, one of the leading figures of the Enlightenment, seeking his advice on rational governance. The point was to use state power to create modern citizens, armies, and national cultures.[19]

Other states became modern by following democratic principles. America and France had democratic revolutions, embracing liberal political values and making the power of the state contingent on the consent of citizens. They emphasized the rights of citizens: liberty, equality, and the right to property. They championed Locke over Hobbes, associating modernity with the struggle against tyranny. England did not have a democratic revolution, but adopted Lockean values to avoid it. Whatever the exact political path, each state pursued a version of modernity, and used culture and infrastructure to embody it physically.

The infrastructures that held states together and defined differences among them were both intellectual and economic. The most important infrastructure for government, according to Weber,[20] was the bureaucratic file. As Patrick Joyce[21] has shown for the 19th century, flows of paperwork, including files, became important to the British state. The Postal Service in particular became a crucial source of national identity and an effective tool of colonial domination (see Figure 4.5).

On the one hand, the Postal Service connected all citizens in Britain, and distributed agents of the state into towns and cities, helping build a visibly national institution.[22] In addition, the Post Office became home to the colonial archives for the Raj in India, mediating between officials in India and Britain. Their negotiations over files allowed them to work out colonial legal policies that were mutually comprehensible in India and Britain.[23]

Industrial policies provided another intellectual infrastructure for nurturing national identities. England and Germany, for example, had distinctive approaches to labor. In

---

[19] James Billington, *The Icon and the Axe: An Interpretative History of Russian Culture* (New York: Random House, 2010), Kindle edition; Nancy Mitford and Liesl Schillinger, *Frederick the Great* (New York: Penguin, Random House, 2013), Kindle edition.

[20] Max Weber, Gunther Roth, and Claus Wittich, *Economy and Society: An Outline of Interpretive Sociology* (Berkeley: University of California Press, 1978).

[21] Patrick Joyce, *The State of Freedom* (Cambridge: Cambridge University Press, 2013); Weber, Roth, and Wittich, *Economy and Society*.

[22] Joyce, *The State of Freedom*, pp. 53–99.

[23] Joyce, *The State of Freedom*, pp. 53–99.

FIGURE 4.5 *Rudolf Ackermann,* The Post Office. *From the Microcosm of London, 1808*

textile manufacture, the English paid workers by time in the factory while the Germans measured the number of things they produced. Both were rational ways of computing labor for factory work, but each tied new forms of manufacture to local practices of compensation.[24]

Transportation infrastructures also had strong effects on national identity, building communities of strangers along different principles that defined group commitments. As Frank Dobbin shows, England, France, and the US all built railroad systems around the same time, but did it in distinctively local ways. In Britain, the contracts went out to individuals, following liberal principles of entrepreneurship. In France, the railroad system was built with a combination of private contracts and government oversight, combining state stewardship with liberal individualism. In the US, policymakers allocated different parts of the railroad system to different entrepreneurs, and reduced their capacity to control land around the railroads by retaining some for the government. This choice reflected American distrust of both public and private authority and the American habit

---

[24] Richard Biernacki, *The Fabrication of Labor* (Berkeley and Los Angeles: University of California Press, 1997), chapter 2.

FIGURE 4.6 *Chinese Railroad Workers, Sierra Nevada Mountains*

of distributing governmental authority to put limits on power.[25] Each country built a railroad system, in other words, using local cultural assumptions to yield a system that citizens could recognize as their own (see Figure 4.6). The infrastructures joined strangers who might never see each other in a national community.[26]

Military institutions and installations added another layer of national infrastructure that produced competing modernities among states. States built technology to suit their own military traditions and patterns of engineering. They rationalized the training and tactics of soldiers, and the design of defenses, developing military schools and engineering training.[27]

Citizens could now see themselves and their heritage in the ways they got mail, were paid for work, traveled by train, or fought in wars. And they could imagine themselves as part of the same community because they could see distinguishing features of national identities in their shared forms of material life.[28]

[25] Frank Dobbin, *Forging Industrial Policy: The United States, Britain, and France in the Railway Age* (Cambridge: Cambridge University Press, 1994); compare to Kristin Surak, *Making Tea, Making Japan* (Stanford: Stanford University Press, 2012).

[26] Benedict Anderson, *Imagined Communities: Reflections on the Origins and Spread of Nationalism* (London: Verso, 1983).

[27] Janis Langins, *Conserving the Enlightenment* (Cambridge, MA: MIT Press, 2004).

[28] Anderson, *Imagined Communities*; Carol E. Harrison and Ann Johnson, *National Identity: The Role of Science and Technology* (*Osiris* series, 24(1)) (Chicago: University of Chicago Press, 2009).

MODERN CITIES

Cities in the 19th century were nodes in networks of manufacture and trade, developing local ways of pursuing progress that fit both their economic situations and modern principles. Manchester, for example, was a center for the British cotton industry that grew with the factory system from the end of the 18th century. By the 19th century, Manchester was a fully liberal city—a place of contractual relations, the pursuit of property, and liberal self-improvement. Workers came to Manchester to sell their labor, and consumers came to its high street to buy whatever they could afford and industry produced. It was a city with warehouses and an exchange, too, where entrepreneurs placed bets on the future value of things they stored or imported.[29]

Manchester also built an intellectual infrastructure for the social improvement of its citizens. The schools, universities, and libraries were often built in neo-gothic style with vaulted ceilings and spires. They resembled churches, and stylistically connected personal improvement to moral purpose (see Figure 4.7).

Manchester was also a sanitary city that developed a conception of modern cleanliness and used standards of public decency and proper self-governance to judge the worth of people. Self-fashioning individuals were expected to govern their bodies and homes according to rules of collective wellbeing. This legitimated treating the poor as backward rather than just penniless.[30]

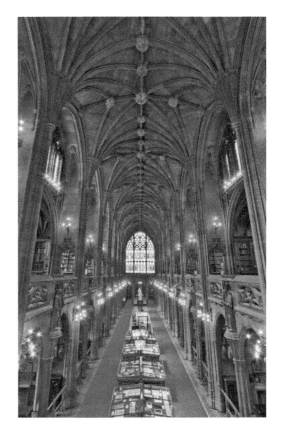

FIGURE 4.7 *The John Rylands Library Reading Room*

Calcutta, now Kolkata, was a colonial city and administrative center in which differences in poverty and standards of decency were even more profound, distinguishing between those groups worthy and unworthy of liberal freedoms (see Figure 4.8). Indians had no property rights and no right to enter into contracts. They could not even get a good education at first. The city was a center of colonial administration, and contributed to the flows of paperwork through the British Post Office. Calcutta famously spawned "babus" or the Indian bureaucrats who worked for the British, adopting Western social practices to claim modernity, but ridiculed by the British for it.[31]

---

[29] Patrick Joyce, *The Rule of Freedom: Liberalism and the Modern City* (London and New York: Verso, 2003).

[30] Joyce, *The Rule of Freedom.*

[31] Krishna Dutta, *Calcutta: A Cultural History* (Oxford: Signal Books, 2003), chapter 2.

VIEW OF CALCUTTA FROM THE ESPLANADE.

FIGURE 4.8 *The Calcutta Esplanade displayed the Two Cultural Worlds in India. Calcutta from the Esplanade, from Robert Montgomery Martin,* The Indian Empire, *Vol. 3, c. 1860*

Calcutta was a trading zone[32]—a site of exchange of colonial power, raw materials, manufactured goods, and liberal ideas—established to further British wealth and world dominance. But it also was home to nationalist intellectuals influenced by liberal thought[33] that decried British tyranny and discussed revolution. These revolutionary intellectuals wanted modern education for Indians to include studying the Vedas along with Locke and Rousseau. This mixing of Indian spirituality and Western reason seemed backwards to the British. Nonetheless, Indian intellectuals established the Hindu College in Calcutta in 1817 as an English language school that taught both European ideas

---

[32] Kapil Raj, "Régler les différends, gérer les différences: dynamiques urbaines et savantes à Calcutta au XVIIe siècle," *Revue d'Histoire Moderne et Contemporaine* (2008), 2: 70–100.

[33] Prithwindra Mukherjee, *Les Racines Intellectuelles du Mouvement d'Indépendance de l'Inde (1893–1918)* (Talmont St. Hillaire: Éditions Codex, 2014).

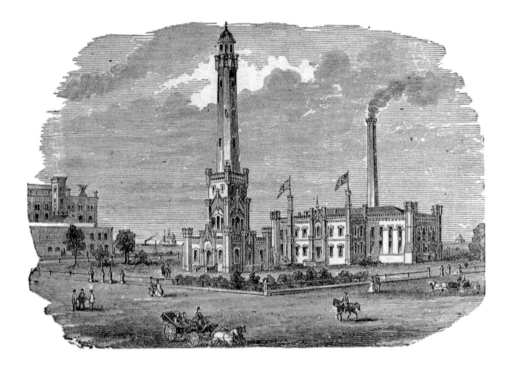

FIGURE 4.9 *Chicago: Engineering an Industrial City from Scratch.* Chicago Water Tower and Pumping Station, 1886

and traditional Indian texts.[34] This version of modernity might have been ridiculed, but the idea of a distinctly Indian modernity made sense in the trading zones of the empire, and was later championed by Gandhi. His nonviolent movement for independence was spiritually consistent with Hindu teachings, and made sense to Indians as a route to self-determination. So, the Indian nationalists of Calcutta in the 19th century helped develop the liberal logic for the Indian drive to independence, but they also connected politics with religion, setting the stage for sectarian violence in Indian politics.[35]

Chicago was a city with no obvious place in global trade because it was far from any major port, but it became a hub by supplying food to cities on America's East Coast (see Figure 4.9). Transforming prairies into grain fields, forests into urban housing, and cattle into meat, it became what William Cronon[36] has called nature's metropolis, changing the environment around it to become a center of trade.

[34] Prithwindra Mukherjee, *Les Racines Intellectuelles du Mouvement d'Indépendance de l'Inde (1893–1918)* (Talmont St. Hillaire: Éditions Codex, 2014).

[35] Gyan Prakash, *Another Reason: Science and the Imagination of Modern India* (Princeton: Princeton University Press, 1999), chapters 3 and 4.

[36] William Cronon, *Nature's Metropolis: Chicago and the Great West* (New York: W.W. Norton & Company, 1992).

THE GREAT UNION STOCK YARDS OF CHICAGO.

FIGURE 4.10 *The Great Union Stockyards, 1876*

The Chicago stockyards became an icon of modern progress because of the scale and efficiency with which they produced meat (see Figure 4.10). The cattle came from surrounding farms, and were fattened in feedlots with grains from fields cut from the prairie. Animals were brought to slaughter in a highly mechanized system, and shipped as meat in refrigerated railroad cars to residents of New York and Boston. The slaughterhouses were, as Kara Wentworth calls them,[37] disassembly lines with a complicated division of human labor as well as chutes and hangers for moving animals and meat.

Chicago also became a center of scientific research with the founding of the University of Chicago, one of the first major universities to focus on the sciences.[38] The city

---

[37] Kara Wentworth, *Performing the Slaughterhouse: Making Knowledge and Difference in Daily Practice* (Dissertation, University of California, San Diego, 2016); Cronon, *Nature's Metropolis*.

[38] John Boyer, *The University of Chicago: A History* (Chicago: University of Chicago Press, 2015), chapter 2.

FIGURE 4.11 *Paris and Modern Urban Sophistication. Gustave Caillebotte,* Paris Street on a Rainy Day, *1877*

depended on natural knowledge to exploit the natural world around it, and needed technological innovations to connect it to the larger political economy. So, it provided the means for its citizens to improve themselves appropriately.

Paris, in contrast, became the symbol of modern urban sophistication in the 19th century with its grand boulevards, elegant *flâneurs*, liberal values, debates over taste, and shopping arcades (see Figure 4.11). It was an international city and a stage for displaying a cosmopolitan modernity.[39]

Paris had become a liberal city with the French Revolution, but not a modern one. Its infrastructure was not appropriate for the industrial era. Even the water supply was insufficient by the late 18th century for the people living in the crowded central city. Something had to be done, and what happened was radical.

Napoleon III asked George-Eugène Haussmann to redesign the urban core of Paris in the 1850s. Haussmann drove broad avenues through the dense, medieval neighborhoods of central Paris, cutting them apart but freeing up circulation and creating vistas within the city. He also extended the city into the suburbs beyond the old city walls,

---

[39] David Harvey, *Paris: Capital of Modernity* (New York and London: Routledge, 2003).

FIGURE 4.12 *The Great Boulevards of Paris. Camille Pissarro,* Avenue de l'Opera, *1898*

forming a much grander metropolis. Haussmann laid out the grand plazas, boulevards, and signature buildings that came to characterize modern Paris, and gave it a new face with Beaux Arts buildings that were widely criticized for their aesthetic conservatism, but were also copied around the world as icons of modern taste (see Figure 4.12).[40]

Paris became a center of fashion in dress and design, a place of shoppers and refined tastes. The pleasures of consumption were celebrated with shopping arcades and by a new modern type, the *flâneur*. This sophisticated gentleman was devoted to wandering the city's streets, arcades, shops, and parks, cultivating and displaying good taste.[41]

---

[40] David Jordan, *Transforming Paris: The Life and Labors of Baron Haussmann* (New York: The Free Press, 1995); David Van Zanten, *Designing Paris: The Architecture of Duban, Labrouste, Duc, and Vaudoyer* (Cambridge: MIT Press, 1987); David Harvey, *Paris: Capital of Modernity* (New York and London: Routledge, 2003).

[41] Gregory Shaya, "The *Flâneur*, the *Badaud*, and the Making of a Mass Public in France, circa 1860–1910," *The American Historical Review* (2004) 109(1): 41–77. In the popular press, the *flâneur* was both celebrated and vilified just as Haussman's work had been. Modernity generated discontent as well as grandeur as promises of progress met the reality of change.

FIGURE 4.13 *Entering the 1900 Exposition through the Tour d'Eiffel. France wiki*

The identification of Paris with cutting-edge modernity was promoted in a number of industrial expositions, most famously the 1889 World's Fair. With the Eiffel Tower as its entrance, the fair exemplified material modernity (see Figure 4.13). It also taught lessons in progress by juxtaposing modest exhibits from Africa and China with the extravagant showcases of industrial capitalism. Taste silently justified modern geopolitical hierarchy.[42]

Other modernizing forces in Paris came from the bottom up. Artists and writers agitated against established principles of modernity. Artists in particular railed against the academies that allowed the state to dictate modern aesthetics, arguing that this practice violated post-revolutionary French values. They made fun of academic art that still focused on classical subjects and forms, including Beaux Arts architecture with its effected evocations of Greece and Rome. They focused more on the beauty and banality of everyday life, and the poetics of color (see Figure 4.14).

To underscore their personal freedom and their distaste for codified principles of modernity, these rebels embraced Bohemian values, and experimented both with new

---

[42] Jill Jonnes, *Eiffel's Tower: The Thrilling Story Behind Paris's Beloved Monument and the Extraordinary World's Fair That Introduced It* (New York: Penguin Books, 2009).

FIGURE 4.14 *A Country Road with Sunlight Playing on the Hills. Camille Pissarro,* Jalais Hill, Pontoiser, 1867

media like filmmaking, and with blends of commercial and independent art.[43] Paris was still a place in which modernity was debated, and ideas of modern progress themselves were put up for scrutiny. It was also a site of material experimentation between art and industry. The combined celebration and critique of modern possibilities in Paris were what made it such an archetype of the modern city.

THE EXPERIMENTAL SELF

Modern institutions of impersonal rule from states to cities to factories flourished with the articulation of modern principles. They were rational means for using resources, including people, so they came to stand for modernity itself. The situation was more complicated for modern selves. They faced the unfreedom of discursive modernity with its

---

[43] Henri Loyrette, Sebastian Allard, and Laurence Des Cars (eds), *Nineteenth Century French Art: From Romanticism to Impressionism, Post-Impressionism, and Art Nouveau,* trans. David Radzinowicz (Paris: Flammarion, 2007).

standards and measures of personal competence. Modern criteria of adequacy were used to justify slavery, the subjugation of women, and the impoverishment of workers. Discursive modernity seemed to undermine human agency while celebrating human rights.

In this context, Romantic poets and artists mourned the loss of human feeling and sensitivity to nature that the pursuit of rational progress ignored, pointing out the inherent irrationality in people and the sublime powers in nature. They championed creativity, personal moral responsibility, and cultural improvisation—qualities of modern selves that discourse seemed to have eclipsed. Bohemians and Romantics both in Paris and elsewhere wanted to go beyond reason in science and rational principles of art and commerce, so they could breathe, feel, and know themselves as flawed and perhaps even unnatural according to modern criteria (see Figure 4.15).

William Blake was one of the early Romantic poets who pushed back against principles of progress. Blake sought to understand the more intuitive knowledge of so-called primitives, and to see the divine in nature—including human bodies and their sexuality.

FIGURE 4.15 *Reverence for the Unspeakable. William Blake, Sconfitta in the Song of Los, 1808*

Blake promoted sensibility over common sense. He asserted that passions were more fundamental and protean than logic, and that nature was more sublime than progress. Blake was convinced human life was characterized by both good and evil, reason and desire, passive contemplation and bodily pleasures. Heaven and hell were joined in the best and worst of life, making human existence a moral paradox.

THE CLOD AND THE PEBBLE

from the Songs of Experience

Love seeketh not itself to please,
    Nor for itself hath any care,
But for another gives its ease,
    And builds a heaven in hell's despair.

So sung a little clod of clay,
    Trodden with the cattle's feet,
But a pebble of the brook
    Warbled out these metres meet:

Love seeketh only Self to please,
　　To bind another to its delight,
Joys in another's loss of ease,
　　And builds a hell in heaven's despite.[44]

Blake wanted to probe human irrationality and feel profound wonder, and so he illustrated his poems with mystical visions to convey the unspeakable powers alive in human earthly existence. His intertwining of words and images was a way to recover the imaginary. Profound knowledge lay between words and pictures, he suggested, rather than in discourse.[45]

Blake was most concerned about the unfreedom of discursive modernity for individuals. He thought anyone who submitted to standards of conduct was not really a self at all.[46] He rejected the idea of human progress, too, and wanted all self-fashioning and self-seeking individuals to be poets—keepers of the word unconstrained by common-sense reasoning.[47] In advocating creative freedom, he sought to recover the capacity for imaginative improvisation of early modernity that had been lost in the face of modern discourse.

There were also scientists who worried about the limits of rationality, and the heteronormativity of the Enlightenment's natural man. Perhaps the most famous was the great chemist, Sir Humphry Davy. Davy was an experimental chemist of international renown, working in the laboratory tradition established by Lavoisier. He used electricity to break down compounds and isolate chemical elements. But he also studied chemicals by taking them as drugs. In a scientific demonstration hall with witnesses present, Davy inhaled laughing gas to make his reactions evidence of what the chemical could do.[48] In this way, he started the tradition of heroic self-experimentation in modern science.[49]

Davy broke standards of modern, rational conduct in his public actions, too, experimenting with what it meant to be a man. He reacted against the modern heterosexual gender compact, and was accused of being a dandy for his ambiguous sexual identity. Instead of acting like a "natural man" in Rousseau's sense, he made himself "unnatural" with his careful attention to appearance and manners—qualities associated with a decadent court society and with trivial women.

So, Sir Humphry Davy along with William Blake helped establish within modernity critiques of modern discourses about rationality and natural man. They recognized the destructive aspect of discursive common sense, and tried to recapture the freedom of modern self-making outside of models of progress.

---

[44] William Blake, *Songs of Innocence and Experience*. Copy B, 1789, 1794 (British Museum) electronic edition. www.blakearchive.org/exist/blake/archive/copy.xq?copyid=sonsie.b&java=no

[45] Alexander Gilchrist, *Life of William Blake* (London: John Lane, 1907), Kindle edition.

[46] Gilchrist, *Life of William Blake*.

[47] Gilchrist, *Life of William Blake*.

[48] Jan Golinski, *The Experimental Self: Humphry Davy and the Making of a Man of Science* (Chicago: University of Chicago Press, 2016).

[49] Naomi Oreskes, "Objectivity or Heroism?" *Osiris* (1996), 11(2): 87–113.

PART TWO

GENEALOGIES OF MODERN SOCIAL TYPES

CHAPTER FIVE

GEOPOLITICS AND DISCOURSES OF RACE

Nowhere has the power and destructiveness of modern discourse been more evident than in race relations. As early as the 15th and 16th centuries, geographers began to comment on the variability of the human groups that they encountered as they traveled. What they wrote about differences was from the start entangled with the geopolitical purposes of their voyages—what European travelers wanted to do in distant lands and with foreign people.

As Londa Schiebinger[1] has argued, racial theories were gendered as well as geopolitical—developed to mediate global relations among men. Race was elaborated along multiple lines to organize and legitimate different forms of domination. The version of race used to justify slave labor in plantations, for example, was not the same as what was used for negotiating trade deals in China or administering the Raj in India. "Knowledge" of others served different situations of power in radically diverse ways. Nonetheless, Europeans still insisted that race was natural not because anyone could prove that racial differences were natural, but because group distinctions could shape relations of power more effectively if they were understood to be real.

"Race" as it is usually described today is both a way of classifying groups as physically distinct types, and a repertoire of cultural imaginaries, addressing the moral qualities of racial groups. Race remains an active part of modern discourse and imagination even though DNA studies show there are no genetic markers to distinguish racial groups as natural kinds. Racial imaginaries persist because they are entangled with ideas of progress

---

[1] Londa Schiebinger, *Nature's Body: Gender in the Making of Modern Science* (Boston: Beacon Press, 1993), chapters 4 and 5. The focus on men and the ambiguity of race together has made intersectionality a problem to analyze. It is easy to question what constitutes intersectionality even though the experience of double exclusion has historical foundation. See Kimberly Crenshaw, "Demarginalizing the Intersection of Race and Sex," *University of Chicago Racial Forum* (1989), 140: 139–67; Jennifer Nash, "Rethinking Intersectionality," *Feminist Review* (2008), 89: 1–15.

and practices of global power. Racial imaginaries are not so easily abandoned even in the face of facts, and they remain reinforced by spatial divisions at both the global and national levels.[2]

European interest in race had started growing in the Renaissance as Europeans traveled, traded, colonized, established plantations, and imposed themselves by force on others around the world, acquiring knowledge of others as they moved. They sought to expand capitalist trade wherever they went, but they tried to do so in different ways. In some places, explorers simply looked for trade routes and resources; in others, merchants set up trading stations; in still others, entrepreneurs established plantations; and when they could, states established colonial administrations to extend their territorial powers. In all of these circumstances, Europeans engaged racial "others," and gathered knowledge about them to consider how they could use or dominate them.

Not all descriptions of racial difference were demeaning even though they all shaped relations of power. If a group was defined as having good character but not cultivating all its land, this was an excuse for taking the land. In this sense, races—even when treated with respect—were never simply natural kinds but rather elements of political analysis.[3]

Europe had a long history of constructing cultural imaginaries of race. Jews had been treated for centuries as money-changers, and corrupting and dangerous barbarians—speaking a different language and engaging in unholy practices. Seen as a tribe or nation apart, Jews were isolated from Christians by patterns of segregation and discrimination that kept Jewish culture strong.[4]

The otherness of Jews made them easy targets. As we have seen, they were attacked during the plague to end God's rage, and they were later expelled from Spain. They were even stereotyped as greedy by Shakespeare for their success in commerce. Still, no one said they were primitive or innocent. They were known for being intelligent, and had incomparable skills in manufacture and trade. So, Jews served as a model race for thinking about groups that were powerful and intellectually sophisticated—like the Chinese or Egyptians. But Jews could not provide precedents for racial imaginaries of "primitives." This meant that new ways of portraying racial others had to be conjured up to justify slave-based plantations and colonial states.

---

[2] George Lipsitz, *How Racism Takes Place* (Philadelphia: Temple University Press, 2011); Claude Steele, *Whistling Vivaldi* (New York: W.W. Norton, 2010); Stuart Hall, *Representation* (London: Sage, 1997); Orlando Patterson, *Rituals of Blood* (Washington, DC: Civitas/Counterpoint, 1998); Lincoln Quillian and Devah Pager, "Black Neighbors, Higher Crime? The Role of Racial Stereotypes in Evaluations of Neighborhood Crime," *American Journal of Sociology* (2001), 107(3): 717–67; Herman Gray, *Watching Race* (Minneapolis: University of Minnesota Press, 2004).

[3] Vincente Rafael, *White Love and Other Events in Filipino History* (Durham and London: Duke University Press, 2000).

[4] Sara Lipton, *Dark Mirror: The Medieval Origins of Anti-Jewish Iconography* (New York: Macmillan, 2014), Kindle edition.

Geographers were at the heart of struggles to understand race because they provided the knowledge base for European exploration, navigation, and geopolitics. Before the 17th century, most geographers focused on the physical form of the earth, particularly the shape of coasts and availability of harbors because this was the fundamental knowledge needed to support seaborne trade. But navigators also worried about the threats posed by local populations or depended on the help locals could offer, and started to make notes on the people that inhabited each part of the world. Having some image of who was out there and what they were like started to seem essential to European expansion by the 17th century. The question was *how* to know others, and what was important to know about groups.

Questions of race became particularly pertinent to Renaissance geographers as they started studying classical geography and reading about Hippocrates' idea that climate was responsible for the different character of racial groups. Human types varied like plants and animals, geographers argued, and mirrored the attributes of the geographical regions they traditionally inhabited. Brutal places made brutal people. Wild lands bred wild people. Temperate climates (Europe) made temperate people. Civilization grew in temperate lands. Once a people gained its character, it was stable and heritable. So, groups could move and maintain their attributes.[5]

In spite of the classical tendency to treat races as natural kinds, many European geographers were Christians, and the Bible said all humans were descended from Adam and Eve. So, geographers faced a fundamental contradiction between classical ideas about the dispersed origins of groups (polygenesis) and the Bible's description of Adam as the single progenitor or forefather of all humans (monogenesis). Did humans share a common ancestor, or did they have many?

Christian geographers tried to resolve the problem by arguing that climate created differences within the one family of man. As the sons of Noah spread around the world after the flood, they developed attributes appropriate to their locales, and their differences were stabilized, becoming heritable traits. This solution made some sense, but raised a troubling question. How could people be shaped by the environment, and then stop responding to it? There was no satisfactory answer, leading comparative anatomists and philosophers in the 18th and 19th centuries to argue that races were different species. But the equation of races to species had a problem, too. Different species could not interbreed and have fertile offspring, but members of different races could. So, in spite of the unresolved questions, both monogenesis and polygenesis persisted as contradictory assumptions about race.

Geographers were not only divided about monogenesis and polygenesis, but also about whether or how to rank races. Some treated each group as distinct, while others thought

---

[5] Benjamin Isaac, *The Invention of Racism in Classical Antiquity* (Princeton: Princeton University Press, 2004), pp. 60–99.

ABORIGINES OF NORTH AMERICA

1 Iroquois 2 Assineboin 3 Crow 4 Pawnee woman 5 Assineboin in gala dress
6 Dakotah or Sioux warrior. 7 Dahotah or Sioux woman.

each race represented a stage of moral or evolutionary development (see Figure 5.1). Which approach they took depended on circumstances. Early explorers and missionaries were concerned about "primitives" and their local knowledge of land. Merchants going to Asia wanted to understand the great civilizations that were gold mines of trade goods. Plantation owners thought about moral differences among the races to justify slavery. And colonial officers assumed the superiority of white races.

It is easy to see in the diversity of approaches to race how European geopolitical interests in different parts of the world drove thought about race, making it a flexible, fluid, and toxic political tool rather than a clear category. The underlying instabilities of race as a category of geopolitics made race an object of scientific study in order to stabilize it. But race never could be found in measures of difference, even DNA, because it was a building block of power, not bodies, that was used by Europeans as they sought to expand their global power.

National identities as well as economies and empires became tied to racial identities, and the colonization of racial others became a measure of national prowess. Racialized nationalism among Europeans began to place importance on racial purity, too, and its maintenance through segregation, deportation, or genocide. The modern liberal subject was racialized as Caucasian, too, defining a racial elite to

Table 5.1 *Different Types of Racial Imaginaries*

	Monogenesis One family of man	Polygenesis Different sources of humanity
Racial Variants	**A. Moral Differences**	**C. Different Temperaments**
Character of races/ racial differences	Primitives or innocents Different moral predispositions Capable of moral reform	Breeding and character Innate abilities and disabilities Natural division of labor
Regions found	N. & S. America, Africa	Africa, Caribbean, S. America, Pacific Islands
Geopolitical goals	Exploration and settlement	Plantation societies
Racial Ranking	**B. Degree of Civilization**	**D. Degree of Evolution**
Capacity to govern wisely	Level of morality or degeneracy Degree of moral discipline	Level of intelligence Rationality of political order
Region found	Egypt, India, China	India, Africa, Australia
Geopolitical goals	Trading relations	Colonial states

distinguish from racial "others" deemed incapable of self-governance and unqualified for liberal freedom.[6]

To get a closer look at the racial classification systems integral to modern geopolitics, I will focus on the four strands of racial thought in European geography. They distinguish races by moral differences, differences in temperament, degree of civilization, and degree of human evolution. The four logics of race are distinct in part because geographers came to disagree about monogenesis and polygenesis, on the one hand, and whether races were naturally ranked or not, on the other. The logics of race were clearly connected to philosophical commitments, but they also varied in relation to European ambitions in particular places. So, racial imaginaries of "others" varied geographically as well as philosophically (see Table 5.1). The relationships are complicated, but we can understand the different logics of race better by looking in more detail at each cell of Table 5.1 and the groups and geopolitical stakes at play in a given racial imaginary.

---

[6] Compare these cultural geographies of race to those discussed in more contemporary examples. George Lipsitz, *How Racism Takes Place*; Michèle Lamont (ed.), *Cultural Territories of Race: Black and White Boundaries* (Chicago: University of Chicago Press, 1999). Seeing racial difference has deeply cultural sources and political implications. See also Alex Manning, Douglas Hartmann, and Joseph Gerteis, "Colorblindness in Black and White: An Analysis of Core Tenets, Configurations and Complexities," *Sociology of Race and Ethnicity* (2015), 1(4): 532–46.

MONOGENESIS AND MORAL DIFFERENCES (CELL A)

Most early explorers and cartographers from Europe were good Christians or Jews, so they believed in monogenesis: the idea that God made the earth, and then created Adam from the earth in God's image. All human beings were sons and daughters of Adam, and were distinguished from animals by their moral capacity to rule other creatures and their duty to God to manage Creation wisely.

Since everyone descended from Adam, racial groups were all part of the same family. This meant that differences among them had to be moral. The 16th-century cartographer and navigator Nicolas de Nicolay[7] described monogenesis in terms familiar for the period, saying:

> The archetype of human being [was] Adam, name signifying land or earth not only because his body was formed from the earth, but more because the earth was given to him for his possession and habitation as monarch of the animals. [While animals] according to their types are confined and limited to particular elements, man [is] seigneur and prince of the whole sphere, both earth and sea. And all climates, all airs and under whatever part of the heavens, man by prerogative from God, his Creator, can live. Such that on all *terra firma*, there is no place without human habitation.[8]

Some explorers saw the people they met as moral innocents, and some missionaries described them as dirty heathens. Most found the groups they encountered as something in between—morally flawed but fundamentally human.

Samuel de Champlain was a typical explorer and monogenesist who grappled with the profound differences between Europeans and Native Americans. He went to North America looking for a northwest passage to Asia. He admired many of the people who served as guides, impressed by their knowledge and generosity. He admitted they could use instruction in Christian values, and he hoped this would do them good. But on his 1612 map (see Figure 5.2), he depicted native couples using conventions of Renaissance painting as Adam and Eve.

With these images, Champlain gave native groups moral standing as children of God. He made New France more appealing, too, by representing it as Edenic. So, he reconciled his ambitions for settling North America with his Christian principles in depicting Native Americans as the equivalent of Adam and Eve.

Many other European geographers, particularly those that never visited the regions they depicted, presented primitives in the Americas as savages to conquer and enslave. They saw European settlement as an opportunity to destroy evil by subjugating those who

---

[7] Nicolas de Nicolay, *Dans l'Empire de Soliman le Magnifique* (Paris: Presses du CNRS, 1989).

[8] Nicolay, *Dans l'Empire de Soliman le Magnifique*, pp. 33–4.

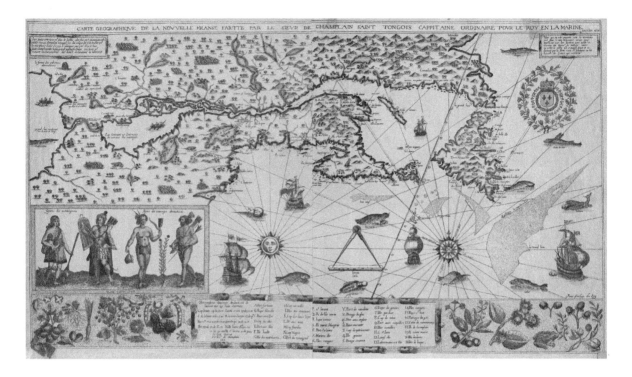

FIGURE 5.2 *Samuel de Champlain, Map of New France, 1612*

were morally corrupt. To emphasize the moral debasement of racial others, they portrayed native groups as cannibals—both in North and South America (see Figure 5.3).[9]

Geographical descriptions of morally degraded types were also used to describe Africa, and used to justify African slavery as early as the 15th century when the Portuguese began taking African slaves to Madeira in the Canary Islands to work on sugar plantations.[10] Gomes Eannes de Azurara, chronicling voyages by the Portuguese to Africa to acquire slaves, described the captured Black Africans as cursed and living without faith. They were, he claimed, like animals without the rational habits of life and decorum of recognizably human beings.[11] In his view, Black Africans were naturally ignoble:

> [T]hese blacks were [slaves], which I believe to have been because of the curse which, after the Deluge, Noah laid upon his son Cain, cursing him in this way:—that his race should be subject to all the other races of the world. And from his race these blacks are descended.[12]

---

[9] J. H. Elliot, *The Old World and the New* (Cambridge: Cambridge University Press, 1970).

[10] Sidney M. Greenfield, "Madeira and the Beginnings of New World Sugar Cane Cultivation and Plantation Slavery: A Study in Institution Building," *Annals of the New York Academy of Sciences* (1977), 292(9): 536–52.

[11] Andrew Valls, *Race and Racism in Modern Philosophy* (Ithaca: Cornell University Press, 2005), p. 25.

[12] Gomes Eannes de Azurara, *The Chronicle of the Discovery and Conquest of Guinea, Vol. I*, trans. Charles Raymond Beazley and Edgar Prestage (New York: Burt Franklin Publisher, 1963), p. 55.

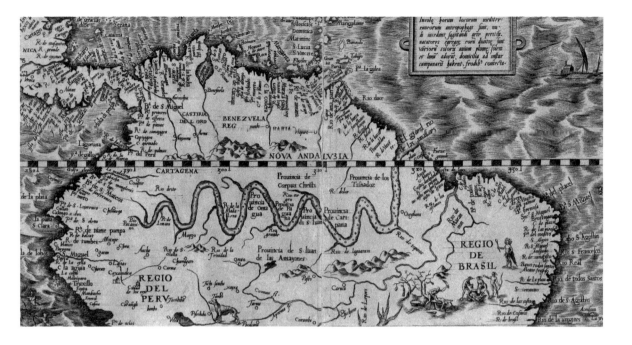

FIGURE 5.3 *Detail of*
Brazil with Cannibals.
Diego Gutiérrez, 1592

Black African slaves were descendants of Adam, but morally destined to servitude.[13]

Monogenesis took a different form when projected onto more powerful groups. Nicolas de Nicolay traveled into the Ottoman Empire in the 16th century when that empire was expanding rapidly into Eastern Europe, and Europeans were terrified that nothing could stop them.[14]

Nicolay was predisposed by conventions of Renaissance geography to see the Ottomans as barbaric and morally degenerate Turks, but he nonetheless wanted to understand how they could be powerful. So he did research. For example, at a dinner for the French ambassador, he noticed a Delli horseman (see Figure 5.4), Delli being the Turkish word for madmen. The horseman was dressed in furs and feathers, and had a wild appearance. He admitted to Nicolay that Dellis looked bizarre, but explained that they were a group of esteemed warriors that had to pass many proofs of valor to wear the array of feathers and furs he had in his costume. His clothing was a badge of honor, he testified.[15]

Nicolay argued that Europeans could also be misled by the fine appearance of some Ottomans. Janissary soldiers (see Figure 5.5), for example, were well-dressed and

---

[13] This moral view of racial degradation legitimated the "social death" of slaves, and the lynching of former slaves. See Orlando Patterson, *Slavery and Social Death: A Comparative Study* (Cambridge, MA: Harvard University Press, 1982), and *Rituals of Blood*.

[14] Nicolay, *Dans l'Empire de Soliman le Magnifique*, pp. 9–24.

[15] Nicolay, *Dans l'Empire de Soliman le Magnifique*, pp. 226–9.

FIGURE 5.4 *Delli Horseman, 1576–7. From Nicolas de Nicolay,* Les Navigations, Pérégrinations et voyages faicts en la Turquie par Nicolas de Nicolay

FIGURE 5.5 *Janissary Soldier, From Nicolas de Nicolay,* Les Navigations, pérégrinations et voyages, etc., *1577*

disciplined men who looked European, but they were in fact dangerous. They were children of European slaves who had been taken away in childhood, and trained in special residences to become fierce and fearless fighters. They were notoriously cruel to their enemies and particularly loyal to the sultan.[16]

The Janissaries confounded Nicolay's belief that races were groups with distinct bloodlines and inherent moral tendencies. The Janissaries were Europeans by blood who were made barbaric by social engineering. Nicolay noted that the Ottomans used residential isolation to manage the attributes of others groups. Jews in the Ottoman world had to live separately in their own communities, and wear yellow turbans to identify themselves. They, too, Nicolay reasoned, maintained group traits because they had been forced to live as a distinct moral community apart from the Turks.[17]

---

[16] Nicolay, *Dans l'Empire de Soliman le Magnifique*, pp. 154–9.
[17] Nicolay, *Dans l'Empire de Soliman le Magnifique*, pp. 233–5.

Whether geographers saw good or evil in racial others, the Christians who believed in monogenesis saw race as a moral category. They attributed the wide variety of human characteristics to moral differences, justifying their fears and admiration of others with moral measures. Missionaries used this idea to justify converting the heathens to Christianity, and slave traders used it to justify keeping some groups in chains. All were children of Adam and capable of leading moral lives, but not all acted morally, and this made it legitimate to subjugate them.

MONOGENESIS AND DEGREE OF CIVILIZATION (CELL B)

The geographers who believed that some races were naturally better than others thought it must be possible to *rank* races, and monogenesists did this according to their degree of civilization. Civilization was translated politically as their capacity for intelligent and virtuous self-governance—a kind of moral fiber visible in their patterns of culture.

Johann Gottfried von Herder described civilizations as rising and falling, so the degree of civilization of any group was part of a historical process. Races would undergo periods of improvement and degeneration—a form of ongoing differentiation of groups he thought had existed since Creation:

> the divine intellect has married unity with the innumerable diversity on earth: only *One and the same species is humankind on earth*. ... the Calmucks and the Negroes remain completely human even in the construction of their head and the Malakulans demonstrate abilities that some other nations do not possess. Nature has provided for each kind and given each one its own inheritance. ... [But] [t]he whole course of a human being's life is transformation ... hence the whole of humankind is engaged in a continuing metamorphosis. Blossoms fall off and wilt; others bloom and send out shoots; the great tree bears all of the seasons on it crown at once ... the Germans were Patagonians a few centuries ago and are no longer so; the inhabitants of future climates will not resemble us. And so human history becomes a theater of transformations that only He can survey who animates all of these constructs and who enjoys and feels Himself in all of them.[18]

Races could decline as well as become civilized, according to Herder. This explained why places that had had important civilizations like Egypt, India, and China had lost some of their greatness. Those races had become degenerate, Herder argued. People in Asia and the Middle East were not racial primitives; they were in moral decline.[19] Herder described the Chinese, for example, as childlike and artificial (see Figure 5.6). They were

---

[18] Robert Bernasconi and Tommy L. Lott, *The Idea of Race* (Indianapolis: Hackett Publishing, 2000), pp. 23–6.
[19] Bernasconi and Lott, *The Idea of Race*, pp. 23–6.

held back intellectually by their pictorial way of writing that sapped their ability to think rationally. They could not create a social contract or scientific civilization in spite of their intelligence.[20] They tried to sell poor quality goods to foreigners, but this was just evidence of their childlike qualities of mind.[21]

Herder's degrading imagery of decadent and childlike others provided a basis for Western distrust of "Orientals".[22] In his mind, the "Orient" was characterized by its decadent and corrupt groups; it was a site of old civilizations filled with beautiful things locals were too depraved to deserve (see Figure 5.7).[23]

Efforts to rank the races in moral terms were means for creating systematic accounts of racial differences, and they were spurred by the development of systematics in the biological sciences. The rankings were also useful for justifying European expropriation of the material riches of foreigners. If others were lower creatures, they did not deserve their riches. In this way, the study of comparative civilizations served commercial as well as political interests.

The French Geographical Society in the early 19th century made the geopolitical implications of comparing civilizations clear with its effort to study colonialism as a civilizing practice. Edme-François Jomard, one of the founders of the Society, convinced fellow geographers to measure degrees of civilization among the races of the world, focusing mainly on primitives and noting the effects of European contact. The geographers would also study ancient societies like Egypt and India and the decline of civilizations. They assumed that the French brought civilization with them wherever they went in the world, and wanted to know where it made a difference.[24] The point was not to appreciate local culture, but improve it with Western contact.

The geographers who ranked civilizations by their morality and modernity wanted to make the concept of race more consistent and stable, but they ended up contributing

FIGURE 5.6 *Anonymous, Stereotype of "Childlike" Chinese People Imitating Western Dress and Life.* China Westernizes, *1830*

---

[20] George Steinmetz, *The Devil's Handwriting* (Chicago: University of Chicago Press, 2007), pp. 400–1.

[21] Michael Palma, Hans Adler, Johann Herder, and Ernest Menze, *Johann Gottfried Herder on World History: An Anthology* (New York and London: Routledge, 2015), Digital edition.

[22] Edward Said, *Orientalism* (New York: Pantheon, 1978).

[23] Bernasconi and Lott, *The Idea of Race*, pp. 24–6.

[24] Martin Staum, *Labeling People: French Scholars on Society, Race, and Empire, 1815–1848* (Montreal and Kingston: McGill-Queen's University Press, 2003).

FIGURE 5.7 *Image of Oriental Splendor and Decadence in a Hammam or Turkish Bath*

to competing views of race. So, race became a more diffuse category, and the problem of explaining racial differences became more intractable.

POLYGENESIS AND DIFFERENCE OF TEMPERAMENT (CELL C)

Polygenesis treated races as comparable to breeds of animals or species with different temperaments adapted to their environment. While monogenesists argued there was a fundamental difference between humans and animals, since all humans were sons of Adam and modeled on God, polygenesists argued that differences among humans were just as profound as those among animals, and were produced by the same natural forces that created differences among species.

Early ideas about polygenesis in Western geography came from classical texts. Ancient geographers and anatomists alike assumed that climate determined character; 16th-century Europeans could not hold such an un-Christian view, but they could teach it as classical geography, and did in atlases combining classical ideas with modern maps.[25]

---

[25] Denis Cosgrove, "Mapping New Worlds: Culture and Cartography in Sixteenth-Century Venice," *Imago Mundi* (1992), 44: 65–89.

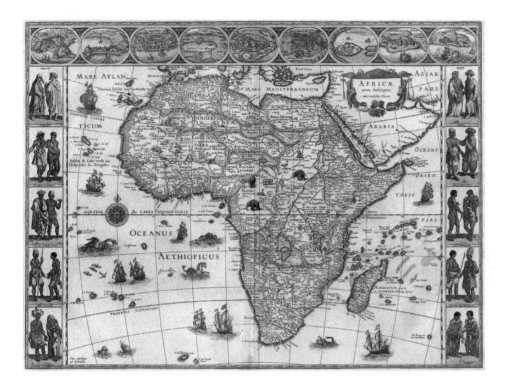

FIGURE 5.8 *Willem Janszoon Blaeu,* Map of Africa, *1635*

Blaeu's *Atlas Maior* was in this tradition. Blaeu associated racial groups with climate zones both on maps and in the text. He wrote that the *ancients* had divided the earth into belts or zones between the poles (latitudes)—five climate belts to match the five divisions of the heavens.[26] To emphasize the connection to race, Blaeu named the zones in South America after groups living at a given latitude: Brazilian, Peruvian, Paraguayan, Chilean, and, at the south tip, savages. He did not argue against monogenesis per se, but *presented* these groups as products of the climate.

Blaeu's map of Africa (Figure 5.8) was similar. It depicted the climate zones and connected them to different races, but it also emphasized the effect of climate on race by depicting groups in the north with lighter skin color than those in the south.

By the late 18th century, secular voices arguing for polygenesis became more common—particularly among comparative anatomists. Marie François Xavier Bichat, for example, connected temperament to race, treating it as an inherited characteristic. He argued that each race had different strengths and weaknesses that created a natural division of labor. Members of each group were meant to do the type of work to which they were suited.[27]

---

[26] Joan Blaeu, *Atlas Maior of 1665*, ed. Peter Van Der Krogt (Köln: Taschen, 2005), pp. 14–15.
[27] Staum, *Labeling People*, pp. 16–17, 37.

The French philosopher Voltaire pushed the idea of natural differences even farther, arguing that races were species just like animals. He wrote:

> None but the blind can doubt that the whites, the negroes, the Albinos, the Hottentots, the Lap-landers, the Chinese, the Americans, are races entirely different. [And] negro men and women, being transported into the coldest countries, constantly produce animals of their own species, and that mulattoes are only a bastard race of black men and white women, or white men and black women, as asses, specifically different from horses, produce mules by copulating with mares.[28]

Voltaire saw this view as a way to secularize thought about human nature, but it also justified systematic breeding and exploitation of races—a view particularly welcome in plantation economies. In the French colony of Saint-Domingue (what would become Haiti), a nobleman, the Baron de Wimpffen, proposed the idea of "manufacturing" mixed races to populate the colony with necessary types. The colonial administrators, Gabriel de Bory and his co-author, Michel-René Hilliard d'Auberteuil, debated whether this was a way to address the weakness of the militia. There were few whites to serve in the militia, so they wondered whether it would be worthwhile to create a militia of mulattos. The point was *not* to purify the races or keep them apart, but to breed the kinds of mixed groups that the administrators wanted. It was the racial imaginary of breeders on plantations (and probably those with sexual interest in slaves) that was justified by doctors and geographers who treated races as natural kinds.[29]

It was a long way from classical climate theory to colonial breeding programs, but the logic of racial difference was the same. Traits were fundamental and natural, and could be inherited through lines of descent. Different races had distinct temperaments—as the ancients said. But talking about natural abilities and a natural division of labor also legitimated racial breeding programs that had clear geopolitical purposes in colonies with plantations worked by slaves. Thinking about breeding slaves as a form of social engineering was a precursor to eugenics: the systematic breeding and culling of racial groups.

POLYGENESIS AND RACIAL SUPREMACY (CELL D)

The polygenesists who thought races occupied different stages in human evolution associated human evolution with the growth of intelligence, and placed Europeans on top of the rankings for their achievements in science. They treated modern progress as an outcome of natural differences, and not something everyone could achieve. And because they took

---

[28] Bernasconi and Lott, *The Idea of Race*, pp. 5–6.
[29] William Max Nelson, "Making Men: Enlightenment Ideas of Racial Engineering," *American Historical Review* (December 2010), 115(5): 1364–91; Sara E. Johnson, *The Fear of French Negroes*. Berkeley and Los Angeles: University of California Press, 2012.

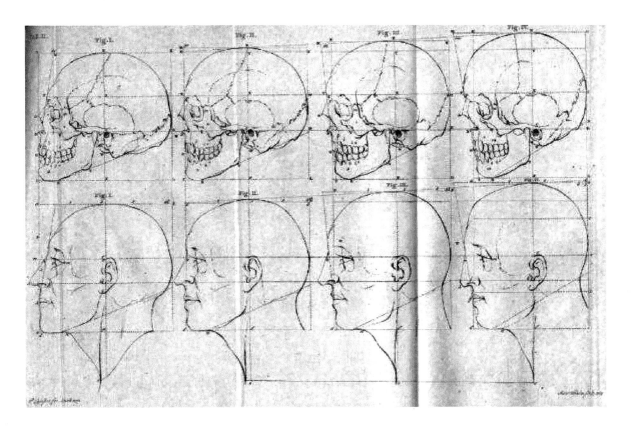

FIGURE 5.9 *Adriaan Gilles, Petrus Camper Facial Angles, 1791*

racial differences to be located in the body, they used skin color and head shape to establish the relative capacity of different races to act intelligently.

Already by the 17th century, François Bernier was arguing for associating racial differences with skin color. In his "new division of the earth," he distinguished among Indo-Europeans, black Africans, Asians, Lapps, and Americans.[30] But by the 18th century, anatomists and doctors thought it more precise to associate race with intelligence, and intelligence with head shape. Petrus Camper, a Dutch physician and physiologist, for example, linked race to facial angles as markers of intelligence (see Figure 5.9).

The French comparative anatomist, Georges Cuvier, in turn, developed his own measures of facial angles, and asked geographers to make measurements around the world to rank all the races systematically on a scale of natural development.[31] The anthropologist Samuel George Morton followed in this tradition, using skull size to distinguish races in buried remains. He took up the descriptive idea of a Caucasian race, and tried to make

---

[30] Bernasconi and Lott, *The Idea of Race*, pp. 3–4.

[31] Staum, *Labeling People*, pp. 28–9, 98, 112.

CAUCASIAN RACE — KURDS, PERSIANS.

1 KURD GIRL. 2. KURD FROM THE PLAIN OF ARARAT. 3 KURD PRIEST. 4 PERSIAN GENTLEMAN. 5. 6 PERSIAN LADY AND GIRL OF TEHERAN.

FIGURE 5.10 *The Caucasian Race: Kurds and Persians. In Blackie and Sons,* Geography

it measurable. Studying skulls in Egypt, he argued that the Ancient Egyptians found in mummies were white rather than black. He did comparative skull measures on groups within the US, too. Whites, he reported, had the largest brains, Americans (natives) had medium ones, and Africans had the smallest.

Similar arguments were made for Caucasian racial superiority (see Figure 5.10). Julien-Joseph Virey and J.-B. Bory de Saint Vincent in France used cranial and facial measurements to argue for the superiority of whites over all non-white people. Virey was the most vitriolic white supremacist, claiming that the facial angle of the orangutan at 65 degrees was close to the 70 degrees of Ethiopians. In contrast, the Japanese facial angle was almost 90 degrees, so Ethiopians were inferior to Asians in "intellect and sociability."[32]

Arthur de Gobineau used a similar understanding of race to explain the decline of great civilizations by interbreeding.[33] Hans Schinz in Africa saw racial mixing as bad for

[32] Staum, *Labeling People*, pp. 40–6.
[33] Bernasconi and Lott, *The Idea of Race*, p. 45.

local groups, too. He warned against trying to reform "Hottentots" since their conversion to Christianity had gained them nothing. They remained naturally repulsive, he contended, and were on the road to extinction because when they tried to imitate the white man, they could not succeed.[34] Any mixing of the races, he thought, put at risk the virtues of a given race and even its viability.

THE LEGACY OF RACIAL IMAGINARIES

The contradictions among these racial imaginaries never diminished the cultural purchase of the racial stereotypes they generated. Racial politics within countries as well as between them depended on the flexibility of racial imaginaries so they could fit new circumstances. But to make race an effective tool of geopolitics and sustain the global order, generation after generation tried to make race discursively real through science.

Slaves could be freed, but this did not strip them of the racial logics of their bondage. Racial imaginaries justified giving natural rights and liberal freedoms only to a few races.[35] Modernity had been defined by Hobbes by its opposite—the primitive that was unworthy to exercise power or enjoy liberal freedoms. By characterizing some races as deficient, geographers helped to sustain European power as natural or an expression of moral order. In this way, race studies made a joke of the Enlightenment concept of natural man as universal because what was natural to men varied, and what men naturally deserved was muddied by patterns of power. Race provided the images of depravity, primitiveness, and incapacity that could explain why some groups could dominate others. The proliferation of racial imaginaries to stabilize relations of global power did not diminish the sense that race had to be natural. And even the discovery that there was no DNA marker of race has not diminished the power of the racial discourses set by early geographers.

---

[34] Steinmetz, *The Devil's Handwriting*, pp. 153–4.

[35] Patterson, *Rituals of Blood*; Lipsitz, *How Racism Takes Place*; Hall, *Representation*.

CHAPTER SIX

PROPERTY, LABOR, AND DISCOURSES OF GENDER

As men were being sorted into races according to their "natures" and male attributes were used to distinguish "nations," women were set apart as not natural at all. Women mattered to nations and races as mothers, apparently acting naturally in bleeding and bearing children. But to become mothers, they needed artifice to attract husbands—charm and physical enhancements of their beauty. Even as mothers, they were asked to suppress their own impulses to devote themselves to developing the natural abilities of their children. In this way, women became unnatural, and innately "other" to modern men who "naturally" pursued their own desires.

Women and men had always been understood as different, but within the modern gender compact, they were complementary opposites rather than comparable kinds. Men used science and industry to make property; women stayed at home to attend to the happiness of their families. Once they were married, women lost independent rights to property and hence the value of their labor. They were social types required for and constrained within heterosexual families—units run by men that integrated economic life and reproduction.

Women who were expected to be frivolous and charming were sometimes happy to do so. Women had inherited the traditions of court society: fashionable dress, leisured cultivation, and the arts of courtesy and charm. Attention to appearances and a willingness to dissemble to please others had been noble attributes previously shared with noble men. Men and women alike at court had cultivated the art of leisure, and performed their high standing. Male courtiers as well as women had put on elegant fashions, taken dancing lessons, and applied makeup. But in the 18th century, men started to shed these habits to fit themselves into Enlightenment ideals of natural manhood and to improve their fortunes through the pursuit of property. This left women with courtly graces, manners, leisure, and fashion, but no power. They became repositories of the artifice and etiquette of European court culture as modern men sought to become natural leaders of modernity.

This vision of men and women as complementary opposites became popular in the 18th century, partly as a reaction against the intellectual power of women in French salons, and partly because of threatening talk about egalitarian marriage.[1] The complementarity thesis described men and women as natural opposites with a necessary hierarchy and purpose as members of patriarchal, heterosexual families.

Rousseau described complementarity this way:

> But for her sex, a woman is a man; she has the same organs, the same needs, the same faculties. The machine is the same in its construction. Yet where sex is concerned man and woman are unlike, each is the complement of the other; the difficulty in comparing them lies in our inability to decide, in either case, what is a matter of sex, and what is not.[2]

FIGURE 6.1 *François Boucher,* Madame de Pompadour, 1756

According to the complementarity thesis, women should be consigned to trivial, mindless activity so they would not overtax themselves. They had silly, little minds to shelter from arenas of money and power. They were unreliable and untrustworthy, too, because they dissembled and did not reason. They were driven by vanity and servility to act in unnatural ways. So, they were not to be trusted with economic or political power (see Figure 6.1).

The complementary thesis did not go unchallenged. There were powerful women and early feminists who spoke against the cruelty and irrationality of treating women as the opposite of men. But medical researchers looking for differences in gendered bodies—like those looking for racial differences in facial angles—found them, and argued from this evidence that women and men were natural opposites, not variants of the same kind.[3]

These differences in gender were embedded in clothing in the 18th century as men and women started to dress very differently from each other. This shift in costuming coincided with the ascendancy of English fashions on the eve of the French Revolution. Anxious gentlemen wanted to forestall a revolution in England by distancing themselves from

---

[1] Benedetta Craveri, *The Age of Conversation*, trans. Teresa Waugh (New York: New York Review of Books, 2005).

[2] Jean-Jacques Rousseau, *Émile* (New York: Heritage Illustrated Publishing, 2014), Kindle edition, p. 231.

[3] Londa Schiebinger, *The Mind Has No Sex? Women in the Origins of Modern Science* (Cambridge: Harvard University Press, 1991), particularly chapters 8 and 10.

A MORNING VISIT—or the FASHIONABLE DRESSES for the YEAR 1777.

FIGURE 6.2 *Woman with a High Wig*

FIGURE 6.3 *William Hogarth,* Mary Edwards, *1742*

the nobility in France. So, landowners on great estates began to dress more simply than women and more like ordinary men.

Women, in contrast, held onto the purses, high heels, ribbons, laces, and wigs of male courtly attire, and continued to wear tight corsets and panniers or side hoops of metal and bone to shape their bodies in a dramatic way (see Figure 6.1). Such forms of courtly artifice had once been marks of power, but the excesses started to be gendered female and make women objects of ridicule (see Figure 6.2).

When women adopted courtly artifice and fashionable dissembling, detaching these attributes from rank and attaching them to gender, they made being a woman performative.[4] Men certainly acted the role of men as much as women performed their gender role, but women were expected to conjure up dreams of modesty and beauty to become objects of desire, and were deemed incapable of anything better than a delightful show. Young ladies learned to maintain a façade, using makeup, clothing, and charm. Being a woman was a way of using body posture, domestic competence, laces, flowers, and piano recitals all in the effort to forge relationships of dependence on men (see Figure 6.3).

---

[4]Judith Butler, *Bodies that Matter* (New York: Routledge, 1993).

GENDERED DIFFERENCES

There had always been differences drawn between men and women, but revisiting gender imaginaries before the 18th century, we can recognize how radical the complementarity thesis was in separating men from women. Prior to the 17th century in Europe, gender was associated with sexuality more than character. Both noblemen and noblewomen thought character was a product of family pedigree rather than gender. Peasants of both genders saw themselves as similar because they lived comparable lives, labored intensively in fields together, and practiced rural crafts at home. In cities, the wives of artisans were often involved in their husbands' shops when they were widowed. So, within each rank, men and women saw themselves as quite similar in character and capacity to one another.

Trade affected gender relations by separating workplaces from homes, producing a distinct culture of domesticity. In the Dutch Republic during the 17th century, men left home for work, and the duties of the household were relegated to women. The result was the formation of dual "spheres": domestic life for women, and work for men.[5] But still members of the same household were understood to be comparable rather than complementary, wearing clothing made with similar fabrics, decorations, and accessories because they were assumed to be moral equivalents (see Figure 6.4).

---

[5] Simon Schama, *The Embarrassment of Riches: An Interpretation of Dutch Culture in the Golden Age* (New York: Knopf, 1987), see chapter 6.

In Spanish and French courts, gender was also divided into spheres. The military duties of men separated them from women. Men were expected to cultivate qualities of bravery and physical prowess that were not demanded of women. But individuals of both genders were disciplined like soldiers in their corselets in Spain, and in the fashionable attire of Louis XIV's court. Noble life in both settings was performance—whether on the battlefield or the public stage at court—to be played with grace and discipline.[6]

So, it was only in the late 18th century when philosophers articulated principles of modernity that men and women were reimagined as opposite in character. Men became natural leaders of the modern world while women became their opposite: carriers of outmoded and artificial traditions of social rank.

NATURAL MAN AND ARTIFICIAL WOMAN

There was more than one way to reimagine gender in modern terms. Feminists advocated more egalitarian relations as more satisfying to both men and women, but the complementarity thesis was championed by Rousseau and associated with his political philosophy. His modern citizen was explicitly a man aided by a complementary wife joined in a heterosexual compact that made other sexualities unnatural and modern politics gendered.

Rousseau wanted to change men, not women, to improve political and social relations. He saw education as the means to do it: "We are born weak, we need strength; helpless, we need aid; foolish, we need reason. All that we lack at birth, all that we need when we come to man's estate, is the gift of education."[7] According to Rousseau, boys were the ones with the natural capacity to improve themselves and become good citizens through education. By stimulating the natural curiosity of boys and giving them the tools to learn about themselves as well as the natural world, they could become men of character able to govern wisely.

Rousseau advocated not teaching boys what to think or do, but rather to learn from experience.

> This education comes to us from nature, from men, or from things. The inner growth of our organs and faculties is the education of nature, the use we learn to make of this growth is the education of men, what we gain by our experience of our surroundings is the education of things.[8]

By teaching according to their capacity to learn and allowing students to cultivate their own interests, Rousseau's pupils could hone their minds, and learn about their own nature.

---

[6]Chandra Mukerji, *Territorial Ambitions and the Gardens of Versailles* (Cambridge: Cambridge University Press, 1997); Jonathan Brown, *Painting in Spain, 1500–1700* (New Haven: Yale University Press, 1998).

[7]Rousseau, *Émile*, p. 6.

[8]Rousseau, *Émile*, p. 6.

Boys would gain strength, he argued, from their independence, and they would be disciplined naturally by experience, comparing what they expected to be true to observations of the world.

Learning for Rousseau was a way to seek happiness. He defined happiness as having the strength to meet one's needs. It was not achieved by becoming rich or powerful, since people with power and wealth only developed new desires and became discontent. Learning how to be happy entailed gaining the ability to satisfy rather than multiply needs. All powers and needs were addressed socially, so happiness required knowing how to contribute to civil society and establish a heterosexual family.

Women, according to Rousseau, had the duty to please their husbands and raise their sons well to do their part for society. This obligation was derived from their nature, but was not a simple reflection of it. They had a capacity for reason but no purpose for it.[9] Girls needed to develop charm and grace to please men, and so could not benefit from the discipline of reason. Women also had no need for freedom or self-determination, Rousseau believed. All people in society had to give up some freedom to live together. Women just had a particular kind of unfreedom; they were unnatural, so they were necessarily kept under surveillance and were subject to the judgments of others.

> A man has no one but himself to consider, and so long as he does right he may defy public opinion; but when a woman does right her task is only half finished, and what people think of her matters as much as what she really is. Hence her education must, in this respect, be different from man's education. "What will people think" is the grave of a man's virtue and the throne of a woman's.[10]

Mary Wollstonecraft objected to Rousseau's arguments about women and education, and made the case for gender equality. She argued that the same education for men should be extended to women. Both had a natural capacity for reason, and needed it to be cultivated. She observed that women were already eagerly reading and debating ideas, but books explicitly for women tended to over-simplify and trivialize complicated subjects like science. So, women could not pursue their education properly. Wollstonecraft argued this made women unhappy and unsettled:

> Women, in particular, are rendered weak and wretched by a variety of concurring causes … [and] their minds are not in a healthy state; for like the flowers which are planted in too rich a soil, strength and usefulness are sacrificed to beauty… One cause of this barren blooming I attribute to a false system of education, gathered from the books written on this subject by

---

[9] Rousseau, *Émile*, pp. 321–414.
[10] Rousseau, *Émile*, p. 328.

men who, considering females rather as women than human creatures, have been [more] anxious to make them alluring mistresses than affectionate wives and rational mothers.[11]

Wollstonecraft echoed Rousseau in arguing that happiness was hindered by dependence and education by authority. What made boys weak were sources of weakness in women. If women were educated well and became happier in life, she argued, they would make better companions in marriage and better teachers of their children. But Wollstonecraft recognized that men like Rousseau were explicitly hindering this possibility. They advocated the subordination of women to meet the needs of men, ignoring altogether the human needs of women.

> I now principally allude to Rousseau, for his character of Sophia is, undoubtedly, a captivating one, though it appears to me grossly unnatural. ... Warmly as I admire the genius of that able writer, whose opinions I shall often have occasion to cite, Rousseau declares that a woman should never, for a moment, feel herself independent, that she should be governed by fear to exercise her natural cunning, and made a coquetish slave in order to render her a more alluring object of desire, a *sweeter* companion to man, whenever he chooses to relax himself.[12]

While Wollstonecraft held out hope that men and women could become equals, Rousseau's heteronormative vision of gender gained the upper hand, particularly after the French Revolution. Court culture had been accepting of male homosexuality and women's intelligence. This was condemned by Reformers such as Rousseau as corrupt. So, as Englishmen fled from court fashions and the danger of revolution, they embraced gender complementarity and the sexual regime associated with it. All that Wollstonecraft worried about started to become reality. Men and women began presenting themselves as naturally opposite, displaying their gender "complementarity".

GENDER, PROPERTY, AND LABOR

The gender culture of the 18th century was associated with property relations that were explored in detail in Jane Austen's novels.[13] There were families in which fathers failed to provide for their daughters, and sons inherited family estates, leaving mothers of young women scurrying to make their daughters attractive to appropriate mates. Often the fate of the whole family and certainly the happiness of mothers were contingent on young

---

[11] Mary Wollstonecraft, *A Vindication of the Rights of Women* (London, 1792; Mineola, NY: Dover Publications, 1946), p. 6.

[12] Wollstonecraft, *A Vindication of the Rights of Women*, pp. 23–4.

[13] Jane Austen, *Pride and Prejudice* (New York: Penguin Classics, 2002); Austen, *Sense and Sensibility* (New York: Penguin Classics, 2003); Austen, *Mansfield Park* (New York: Penguin Classics, 2003).

ladies pairing with suitable husbands. Gender relations were property relations, and marriages were the only contracts truly important to the "happiness" of women.[14]

John Locke outlined some principles for this property regime. He argued that women were not in themselves property, and could form contracts the same as men. The marriage contract had to be equally entered into even if it defined husbands as masters of their wives. Single women had rights to hold and inherit land independently. But married women could not have separate property unless they were granted an exception. Both women and men were equally in charge of raising children and caring for their welfare because, although men were heads of families, women put labor and even their bodies into bearing and raising children. The family was the bedrock of society and the site of women's power, but it was an institution of property and labor that was necessarily dominated by men. Patriarchs controlled familial wealth, and sons inherited it, leaving women seeking husbands to remain solvent and exercise domestic powers.[15]

Women with their trivial interests and lack of worldliness were defined as better suited to be mothers than managing property. They could only govern the household and raise the children. So, while women could in principle use labor to gain property and make contracts, they had few opportunities to do this.[16] The control of family wealth by men— by gender culture and family law—made heads of household the only truly legitimate economic actors in modern life. The leisure of women and children in a family brought honor to the head of household.[17]

The interplay of gender culture and property relations is visible in family portraits from 18th-century England, such as the Gwillym family portrait by Arthur Devis (see Figure 6.5). The family is painted assembled on a huge lawn in front of their manor house. They are a family of property. But gender matters, too. The painting is entitled "Robert Gwillym of Atherton and Family." Robert is the only one worth naming because he is the proprietor; the others are dependents. Robert and his eldest son are physically set apart from the women and children, their dark clothing blending into the trees behind them. They are one with their nature, and apart from family dependents. The wife and her daughters, in contrast, stand out from nature in their bright colors, and are positioned with the younger sons on the opposite side of the lawn. What appears to be the portrait

---

[14] For example, the resolution of marriage contracts is Mrs. Bennet's only purpose in *Pride and Prejudice*, and the tension between propriety and feeling is worked out contractually. Austen, *Pride and Prejudice*.

[15] Mary Lyndon Shanley, "Marriage Contract and Social Contract in Seventeenth-Century English Thought," in Nancy Hirschman and Kirstie McClure (eds), *Feminist Interpretations of John Locke* (University Park, PA: Pennsylvania State University Press, 2007), chapter 1.

[16] Gordon Schochet, "Models of Politics and the Place of Women in Locke's Political Thought," in Hirschman and McClure (eds), *Feminist Interpretations of John Locke*, chapter 4.

[17] This constellation of power within families and its relationship to the competition among elite families is well described by Thorstein Veblen in the 19th century in *The Theory of the Leisure Class: An Economic Study of Institutions* (New York: Viking Press, 1945).

FIGURE 6.5 *Arthus Devis,* Robert Gwillym of Atherton and Family, c. *1746*

of a dead child is in the middle. In this family, reproduction and property join men to women, but only as complements to each other.

The men on the left are standing, active agents of their own lives; the wife sits, unable to act on her own behalf. She looks up at her husband, as though looking for leadership. The men do not return the gaze. The two gender cultures are clearly presented here as opposite—one natural, one unnatural, one in charge and the other dependent. And the family as a whole is painted as a unit of property and procreation, pertaining to the patriarch and first son.

GENDER CULTURE AND INDUSTRIAL LABOR

With industrialization, the gender split was even more systematically used to regulate property relations. The factory system separated work from home, helping to reduce the power of the family as a productive unit, and reinvigorating the culture of domesticity that separated men who worked from women who raised children and maintained the home. Masculinity was defined less by family and more by labor and property; men were producers in homosocial worlds. Women were supposed to stay home.[18] Even in the 20th century politicians arguing against women's suffrage were still saying:

> Let [woman] teach her daughters that modesty, patience, and gentleness are the charms of women. Let her teach her sons that an honest conscience is the man's first political law. The men are able to run the government and take care of the women. As long as woman is woman and keeps her place she will get more protection and more consideration than man gets. When she abdicates her throne she throws down the scepter of her power and loses her influence.[19]

Sanford in the quote above describes the political implication of complementarity. Women should accept their role as mothers within a separate sphere of domestic power rather than demanding to be citizens worthy of rights. Unconsciously alluding to the roots of femininity in court culture, he suggests women rule from a throne and wield power through their scepter. Their influence derives from their nobility of spirit, and going into politics would diminish it. He presents the state as a patriarchal authority with good intentions toward women. So, women should embrace their God-given role as mothers and homemakers, and stop seeking power beyond what is natural to them.

Through the 19th century, the complementarity thesis dominated women's lives, even if they worked in factories. So, women in rural cotton mills often lived in dormitories to keep them sheltered, marriageable, and dependent. In cities, single women who worked in offices, department stores, and scientific laboratories had more personal freedom, but at work, they were given mindless tasks like sewing, secretarial work, and mathematical calculation—activities that were considered too tedious for active men. Working women earned money, giving them pleasurable but unsanctioned autonomy. But they were measured by their gender culture—their modesty rather than their work, and their role as consumers rather than producers. Labor and property, in principle, belonged to men.[20]

The gender imaginary of men as primarily producers, gaining dignity and wealth from their labor, started to be marked in clothing. Men started to dress in suits—a work costume that identified men of all social ranks as producers. Elite men even wore stovepipe

---

[18] Rosalind Williams, *Dream Worlds: Mass Consumption in Late Nineteenth-Century France* (Berkeley and Los Angeles: University of California Press, 1982).

[19] J. B. Sanford, "Argument against Women's Suffrage, 1911." Prepared by J. B. Sanford, Chairman of the Democratic Caucus. Argument against senate constitutional amendment no. 8. http://sfpl.org/pdf/libraries/main/sfhistory/suffrageagainst.pdf

[20] Kathy Peiss, *Cheap Amusements: Working Women and Leisure in Turn-of-the-Century New York* (Philadelphia: Temple University Press, 1986); John Berger, "The Suit and the Photograph," in Chandra Mukerji and Michael Schudson (eds), *Rethinking Popular Culture* (Berkeley and Los Angeles: University of California Press, 1991), pp. 424–31.

hats (see Figure 6.6) and shiny fabrics for their suits that made them look like their factories.

Their head coverings stood in strong contrast to that of women. By the middle of the 18th century, women were putting up their hair in elaborate styles or wore fantastic hats. Rather than producers, they were objects of fantasy and fantastic in form and bearing. Fantasy was alluring and deemed dangerous to men, as women's bodies were both hidden and dramatically staged (see Figure 6.7). Women were temptresses as often as they were queens.

In this regime of fashion and sexuality, women were both natural and unnatural. Men in stovepipe hats looked like factories while women wearing feathers, flowers, and bright colors looked like birds or meadows. Women were now wild nature—mammals, after all—that used their breasts to feed their young. So, as much as women remained masters of artifice in the 19th century, they they were dressed to look like nature that industrious men could turn into property.

With industrialization, men were joined as producers of modernity in a masculine identity that spanned social classes, and helped build solidarity between workers and those who hired them to work. Men were joined by contracts that regulated production, creating communities of strangers at work. And while contractual labor systematized domination, masculinity helped obscure class differences by associating manliness with the qualities of working men. Men of all ranks were supposed to be hard working, tough, and resilient. They were "risk takers": working men took physical risks in building bridges, forging steel, and building skyscrapers, and elite men took financial risks, investing in factories, engineering schemes, and trade.[21] Building industries and cities together was heroic and masculine work that exemplified the rationality, risk-taking, determination, and daring that made men naturally superior to and distinguishable from women (see Figure 6.8).

Associating masculinity with characteristics of working men helped to make gender a compensatory culture. Workers that had lost autonomy and power in leaving farms for industrial work were now celebrated for their endurance, and physical and technical skills. They were the ones to make things work. This vision of gender attributes offset class divisions among men. So, gender masked patterns of exploitation.

FIGURE 6.6 *Men in Stovepipe Hats*

---

[21] Reece Peck, "You Say Rich, I Say Job Creator," *Media Culture and Society* (May 2014), 36(4): pp. 526–35.

FIGURE 6.7 *Unnatural
and seductive women.*
Toulouse-Lautrec,
Moulin Rouge,
1892–1895

Male gender solidarity was played out through amateur athletics. Elite men started teams and leagues to play sports with one another, becoming more fit like working men by exercising their bodies. But working men often remained better athletes, so they started to be invited to join sports teams (see Figure 6.9). In this way, athletics became a site where masculine virtues were performed for pleasure, but created bonds among men.[22]

For men, the gender system was bottom up and integrating across classes. But for women, gender ideals based on court culture were top-down—alienating elite from working women. Working women fit badly into the gender system, and suffered more from criticism about how they performed their roles. Ladies of means cultivated leisure virtues like manners and taste. But poor women had little leisure, and even less money to care

[22] Gunther Barth, *City People: The Rise of Modern City Culture in Nineteenth-Century America* (Oxford: Oxford University Press, 1980).

FIGURE 6.8 Workers on the Brooklyn Bridge. Dover collection

about manners and the latest styles. Women were not only judged by elite values, but most were also unable to realize them.[23]

What women of all classes shared, however, was a love of artifice. They were shoppers who used clothes to express their social standing and exercise knowledge of fashion, and they used makeup and hairstyles to play with their gender performances. Working mothers could buy magazines with patterns for making the latest styles of clothing for themselves and their children, keeping up to date more or less. But single women with factory jobs started dressing in ways that rejected the hierarchical system of fashion, adopting some elements of dress from the prostitutes to distinguish their attire from high fashion.[24] Being slutty was a political act of defiance.

Women's magazines tried to create a shared gender culture for women around domesticity, providing cooking tips, canning advice, child-rearing ideas, and the like.

---

[23] Peiss, *Cheap Amusements*, chapter 7.

[24] Peiss, *Cheap Amusements*, chapter 7.

FIGURE 6.9 *New York Knickerbockers, Working Man's Team, 1862*

They told stories about women, and contained advertisements about where to buy and how to choose household goods. They defined the culture of domesticity as common to all women, but they also taught manners and taste, reinforcing class distinctions within women's gender culture.[25]

By making consumption and taste so central to their gender culture, women confirmed the importance of what men did as producers, elevating the cultural value of masculinity while also embodying virtues that men did not desire in themselves. It was an effective system of biopolitics because it produced men who worked hard and women who raised children.

The top-down gender of femininity and the bottom-up gender of masculinity made women and men within a given class oddly foreign to each other. Working-class women, for example, were more aspirational than working-class men, wanting the "better things" that fashion dictated from the top. Working men gained dignity just from having jobs and saw no need to put on airs.[26] Elite women, on the other hand, with their concerns about taste and manners, seemed trivial and constraining to elite men who had access to the larger world. Elite men, in turn, seemed too rough to elite women of polite society who

---

25 Peiss, *Cheap Amusements*, chapter 3.
26 Michèle Lamont, *The Dignity of Working Men* (Cambridge, MA: Russell Sage Foundation, 2000).

tried to reform them. In these ways, and others, gender became a difference that seemed almost unbridgeable.

Of course, there were bohemian circles where these gender imaginaries were questioned, and women took off their corsets and donned bloomers so they could move however they wanted. Orientalism became fashionable, and bohemian women got comfortable in caftans and turbans. And women like Margaret Fuller began to argue for women's equality on new grounds: social justice. She connected her views about justice for women to her opposition to slavery. Forms of subjugation, she argued, were an abomination in a free society. She wrote:

> Though the national independence be blurred by the servility of individuals; though freedom and equality have been proclaimed only to leave room for a monstrous display of slave-dealing and slave-keeping; though the free American so often feels himself free, like the Roman, only to pamper his appetites and his indolence through the misery of his fellow being; still it is not in vain, that the verbal statement has been made, "All men are born free and equal." There it stands, a golden certainty wherewith to encourage the good, to shame the bad.[27]

Margaret Fuller went on to argue that working men were deceived by the gender compact. She thought they would begin to recognize the injustices against women when they recognized their own subordination to elite men. "As men become aware that few men have had a fair change, they are inclined to say that no women have had a fair change."[28]

Arguments about freedom from tyranny continued to be voiced by women. And strikes in factories periodically drove wedges between working men and their bosses, making a joke of masculine solidarity. Modern principles of freedom and citizenship were at odds with the modern gender compact, so it was routinely contested even as it remained dominant.

Fuller was an optimist to think that calls for social justice would unite men and women. For many men, gender inequalities were advantageous. And for men without much property, often the greatest comfort in their lives came from their sense of gender superiority: knowing that at least they were not women. The compensatory power of that thought as well as the economic interests of elites kept the modern gender compact surprisingly stable even as women gained rights, gained education, and excelled in sports. Gender solved problems of political economy within industrial capitalism, so gender imaginaries carried more importance than might be expected and extended well beyond questions of physical difference.

---

[27] Margaret Fuller, *Woman in the Nineteenth Century* (New York: Greeley & McElrath, 1845), p. 174. https://archive.org/details/womaninnineteent1845full

[28] Fuller, *Woman in the Nineteenth Century*, p. 156.

CHAPTER SEVEN

THE ASCENT OF MAN AND DISCOURSES OF CHILDHOOD

Efforts to define race and gender differences as natural bases for subordination remained contentious because there were multiple contradictory assertions about the character of races and genders. In contrast, children were successfully defined as natural dependents who needed to be cared for by adults as they developed in stages from primitive babies to rational adults (see Figure 7.1). Children had not always been seen this way. Before modernity, children were mostly seen as small adults. And as modernity developed, descriptions of childhood gained many variants—as divergent as conceptions of race. It seemed as though childhood would remain a contentious category, but theories of child development successfully naturalized diverse conceptions of the child, attributing different characteristics to children as they matured.

Developmental theories did not so much displace older and contradictory views of children. Each conception of the child was located in a transitory phase of maturation. So, developmental theories were able to absorb the cultural contradictions in the category of childhood with narratives of stage-wise progress by children, recapitulating in the life of any given child the stage-like progress of "civilization" from

FIGURE 7.1 *Charles Haigh-Wood, Story-Time, 1892*

primitive to modern. It was a triumph of modern culture, science, and geopolitics.

This model of natural child development seemed supported by evidence. As they matured, children grew from uncontrolled, unreasonable babies to reasoning adults, gaining the moral discipline and intellectual skills to be civilized. This view of children seemed benign, as it held out the promise that all children, if properly treated, could become modern. But the model of child development naturalized the ascent of man, and

FIGURE 7.2 *Albert Anker,* Girl with Dominoes, c. *late 18th century*

defined children who developed in non-normative ways, including doing badly in school, as unnatural or of lower human worth.

Children in developmental theories became gender neutral as well as racially unmarked. The shifts were manifested in children's books and games (see Figure 7.2). The Blackie and Sons annuals in the 19th century had different volumes for boys and girls, but in the early 20th century, the publisher started putting out gender neutral editions. Children in fairy tales from the 19th century were increasingly depicted as animals (natural), so they could be of any race. The stages of childhood stood for human evolution as a whole, and were taught to parents as such in parenting magazines and other media.[1]

While developmental childhood was in principle egalitarian, in practice, it "naturally" reproduced and naturalized class, race, and gender hierarchies. Differences in schools, teaching tactics, and neighborhood cultures produced disparities of achievement that mirrored geopolitical hierarchies. Natural childhood provided a basis for claiming these differences to be natural, making full adult rights and dignity a privilege for the few.[2]

MODERN VERSIONS OF CHILDHOOD

Children had existed in all historical periods, but childhood was a modern invention—a counterpart to modern selves. Before the Renaissance in Europe, children were viewed as not so different from adults. Babes in arms were distinguished from children who could act more independently. But in many places, children that could walk and talk were simply treated as small adults, just lacking skills, size, and strength. Childhood became a distinct category when adulthood required preparation.

According to Neil Postman,[3] childhood started in the Renaissance when nobles at court took learning seriously, studying science and reading history. Children of privilege

---

[1] Nicholas Sammond, *Babes in Tomorrowland: Walt Disney and the Making of the American Child, 1930–1960* (Durham: Duke University Press, 2005); Karin A. Martin, "Becoming a Gendered Body: Practices of Pre-Schools," *American Sociological Review* (1998), 63(4): 494–511.

[2] Barrie Thorne, "'Childhood': Changing and Dissonant Meanings," *International Journal of Learning and Media* (2009), 1(1): 1–9; Myra Sadkar and David Sadkar, *Failing at Fairness* (New York: Touchstone Books, 1994); Paul Willis, *Learning to Labor: How Working Class Kids Get Working Class Jobs* (New York: Columbia University Press, 1981).

[3] Neil Postman, *The Disappearance of Childhood* (New York: Delacorte Press, 1982), chapter 1.

FIGURE 7.4 *Jan Steen,* Feast of Saint Nicholas, *1663–5*

FIGURE 7.3 *Bronzino,* Portrait of a Girl with a Book, *1545*

were expected to become literate to be capable adults (see Figure 7.3). Childhood education did not extend beyond court society, though, because literacy was rejected as too dangerous for peasants who were better off not thinking independently. So, childhood started out as a privilege, and a time to reproduce marks of privilege.[4]

Childhood spread during the Reformation to Protestant children of all ranks. Adults and children alike were taught to read—particularly in rural literacy drives. Children were seen as in need of moral formation, and for this, they were expected to learn to read the scriptures. For Dutch Protestants, the home served as a retreat in which children could be properly disciplined and morally educated before entering adult life. Childhood was not a time to master noble attributes, but instead, to gain moral self-control, learning from patriarchal authorities the moral significance of the scriptures (see Figure 7.4).[5]

---

[4] Postman, *The Disappearance of Childhood*, chapter 1.

[5] Kenneth Lockridge, *Literacy in Colonial New England* (New York: Norton, 1974); David Cressy, "Literacy in Pre-Industrial England," *Societas* (1974), 4(2): 229–40; Katherine Pandora, "The Children's Republic of Science in the Antebellum Literature of Samuel Griswold Goodrich and Jacob Abbott," ed. Carol E. Harrison and Ann Johnson, *Osiris* (2009), 24(1), 75–98.

In Adam's fall
We sinned all.

Thy life to mend,
This Book attend.

The Cat doth play,
And after slay.

A Dog will bite
A thief at night.

An Eagle's flight
Is out of sight

The idle Fool
Is whipt at school.

As runs the Glass,
Man's life doth pass.

My Book and Heart
Shall never part.

Job feels the rod,
And blesses God.

Proud Korah's troops
Were swallowed up.

The Lion bold
The lamb doth hold.

The Moon shines bright
In time of night.

FIGURE 7.5 *New England Primer*

In New England, children were taught how to read using primers that contained rhymes with moral teachings (see Figure 7.5). Intellectual skills were fundamentally connected to social goals. Getting an education in this context was necessary discipline for untamed souls, helping children to take control of their lives and moral destinies.[6]

Children needed careful education and supervision because in Protestant imaginaries, they were more vulnerable to the devil than adults. They could infuse public life with evil with their wild moods and imaginings, so keeping them physically apart for instruction was important to communities as well as to the children themselves.

In the 17th and 18th centuries, childhood began to be distinguished from adulthood with material culture. Children were not only given special books like primers, tailored to their needs, but also special toys, furniture, and nurseries—first at court and then in the urban middle class. Ariès[7] contends that noble children in France started to be kept in nurseries after they were babies. They had tutors in different subjects, and toy soldiers with which to play war games. Under Louis XIV, the *Menus Plaisirs du Roi* provided mechanical toys and small furniture for the king's progeny, and arranged for

---

6 Lockridge, *Literacy in Colonial New England*.

7 Philippe Ariès, *Centuries of Childhood: A Social History of Family Life*, trans. Robert Baldick (New York: Knopf, 1962).

comedians and puppeteers to entertain young members of the royal family (see Figure 7.6).[8]

In Britain as well as France in the 18th century, children became a consumer category with an array of goods addressing their special attributes and needs. Parents could buy their children small desks, books, clothes, toys, and special clothing. They also had toy soldiers and fashion dolls to help children rehearse gender roles in imaginative play (see Figure 7.7). Middle-class children were also held apart from public life— consigned to nurseries and schools. Dedicated physical spaces kept children in the company of nurses and teachers to appear only briefly among adults in genteel homes where they were sources of entertainment. On these occasions, they would show off skills such as reading aloud or playing the piano. Children were like pets more than adults[9]—lumped together with domestic animals with charming skills and affection.

By the late 18th century under the influence of Rousseau, children were seen as naturally curious and innocent. They were now kept apart from adults to protect them. Adults were redefined as a corrupting influence on children, not vice versa. Children had natural virtue that could be preserved by keeping them away from bad influences.[10] Childhood was a time for children to develop their natural capacities—appropriate to the nature of their gender.

The Industrial Revolution expanded the commercial culture of childhood, but also spurred concern about the welfare of children. The mass production of toys like mechanical banks, tin soldiers, and paper dolls allowed more children to play with things deemed appropriate for them. But the growth of industrial cities also made the adult world more dangerous to children, and raised concerns about working-class children for the first time. The industrial uses of child labor made vivid the contrast in the ways of life between rich and poor (see Figure 7.8). Children of all classes, social reformers now argued, needed to be protected and sent to school. This was the only way to give children a chance to realize their full potential as modern individuals and future citizens.[11]

FIGURE 7.6 *Child's Chair and Toys. Jean Siméon Chardin, From Prayer before Meal, 1744*

---

8 Jérôme de La Gorce, *Dans l'Atelier des Menus Plaisirs du Roi. Spectacles, Fêtes et Cérémonies aux XVIIe et XVIIIe Siècles* (Paris: Archives Nationales-Versailles, Artlys, 2010).

9 Neil McKendrick, John Brewer, and J. H. Plumb, *The Birth of a Consumer Society: Commercialization of Eighteenth Century England* (Bloomington: Indiana University Press, 1982), pp. 286–315.

10 Jean-Jacques Rousseau, *Émile* (Heritage Illustrated Publishing, 2014), Kindle edition.

11 Viviana Zelizer, *Pricing the Priceless Child: The Changing Social Value of Children* (Princeton: Princeton University Press, 1994).

FIGURE 7.7 *William*
Hogarth, Tea Party,
1730

Each of these cultures of childhood was a moral regime, and so they were normative and political in character. But in the 20th century, they were incorporated into theories of child development that were defined as descriptive. Children were sometimes devilish, sometimes curious, sometimes in need of protection, and sometimes able to acquire skills. So, natural childhood embedded in stages of development contradictory conceptions of the nature of the child.

DEVELOPMENTAL CHILDHOOD

Childhood was naturalized in the 20th century by philosophers of education who debated educational practices, and by psychologists who studied human development as a sequence of stages. The question for these scholars was not whether development was natural, but how it worked and how to turn natural children into successful adults through schooling.

FIGURE 7.8 *Glass Factory Worker, 1911*

Eric Erikson[12] tied human development to psychodynamics. He contended that people of all ages, not just children, were driven by widely different needs, interests, and desires as they moved through the life cycle. In his theory, learning was not a way to gain a set of socially relevant skills, but to address the yearnings of people, allowing them to make peace with themselves, and then to move on to resolve the next set of life issues. Maturation in this view was a process of addressing emotional needs that changed at different stages.

Jean Piaget,[13] in contrast, focused on cognitive processes of maturation, and associated learning with physical maturation. According to Piaget, in the first two years of life, babies learned mainly by sensory experience. Toddlers later developed skills by acting on the world and seeing the results, but they were not yet able to integrate fully what they learned in different situations. Elementary school children began to reason about things and relations among them, but only about things familiar to them. Finally, around age 12, children developed self-consciousness, and with it, the capacity for abstract thought. Through this natural process, children gained the ability to fashion their own identities

---

[12] Eric Erikson, *Childhood and Society* (New York: Norton, 1950).

[13] Jean Piaget, *The Early Growth of Logic in the Child* (London: Routledge and Kegan Paul, 1959); Howard Gardner, *The Quest for Mind: Piaget, Levi-Strauss and the Structuralist Movement* (Chicago: University of Chicago, 1981).

and determine their trajectories through life, finally recognizing themselves as part of wider social and cultural fabrics.

In these and other versions of child development, children would naturally transform themselves to become rational social actors. Psychologists generally agreed that babies were needy and willful, acting on primitive instincts without concern or real knowledge of others around them. They were driven to attach themselves to their caregivers in order to survive, and then faced the problem of gaining independence. Toddlers started to assert their will and see things they wanted. If frustrated in achieving their desires, they could turn wild and have tantrums—seemingly possessed by the devil or deep emotion. In the struggle to gain autonomy, they learned to control their emotions better, and to use imaginative play to experience what they wanted. School children were more disciplined, and could learn to study the world around them, and begin to see it as a whole. But they only "matured" after they gained the capacity for abstract thought and reflexivity about their own actions. At this point, they were no longer primitive, but could act as modern self-fashioning individuals.

The educational philosophers linked developmental models to ideas about classroom learning steeped in earlier cultures of childhood. John Dewey[14] advocated child-centered learning, meaning careful attention to the period when a child was prepared to learn something new. He assumed like Renaissance parents that children lacked the skills to function as adults, but he also believed like Rousseau that children had an inner curiosity and distinct needs addressed best with natural and experiential education. Dewey understood school-age children as both lacking in skills and in need of individuation, so he wanted to nurture their free will and curiosity, using structured activities that could shape their intellectual growth (see Figure 7.9).

Maria Montessori[15] thought that children learned mainly by experience and designed educational environments filled with puzzles and games adapted to their needs. Since urban children could not safely explore the natural world as Rousseau's Émile had done,[16] she provided indoor environments that were just as educational. In them, children could explore interesting objects at their own pace to advance their thinking as it became appropriate. The program was a logical continuation of 18th-century interest in experiential education and the natural curiosity of children. But she assembled artifacts and used spaces to address the distinctive needs of children at different stages of development, providing a repertoire of tools for engaging in age-appropriate activity.

The Russian psychologist Vygotsky[17] addressed both the inner and public lives of children. Like Protestant teachers, he saw education as socialization, and a kind of moral

---

[14] John Dewey, *Experience and Education* (New York: Free Press, 1997).

[15] Maria Montessori, *The Secret of Childhood* (New York: Ballantine Books, 1982).

[16] Rousseau, *Émile*.

[17] L. S. Vygostky, *Mind in Society: The Development of Higher Psychological Processes*, ed. Michael Cole (Cambridge: Harvard University Press, 1980).

FIGURE 7.9 *Mental Development and Education, 1921*

formation—not just learning skills. As children played with objects, read stories, and took on social roles, he argued, they naturally acquired abilities appropriate not only to their age but also to their culture. Vygotsky treated learning as necessarily sequential as Rousseau had suggested because it was a form of social and cultural learning as well as cognitive development. Children needed certain skills to "scaffold" more complex forms of thought, learning in stages to become a functioning member of society. In this way, his program put Rousseau's ideas in a sociopolitical context.

Rudolf Steiner[18] was the one who explicitly tied child development to the ascent of man. He was primarily concerned with the moral formation of children, and like Rousseau, believed in allowing students to follow their interests and develop their creativity to gain personal resilience and moral integrity. But Steiner thought this open way of learning was done best in stages, exposing children in sequence to stages of civilization. Children needed to explore preliterate forms of culture like music, dance, and art before learning to read, so they could acquire the virtues of oral culture like memory and creativity. He emphasized experiential learning, too, going into nature to learn from it as people had

---

[18] Rudolf Steiner, *Intuitive Thinking As A Spiritual Path: A Philosophy of Freedom*, trans. Michael Lipson (Hudson, NY: Anthroposophic Press, 1995).

done throughout human history. In this way, Steiner created a model of child development explicitly paralleling the development of civilization.

Nic Sammond[19] argues that parents were recruited in the 20th century into the program of raising natural children by learning to act as scientific observers of their progeny and following their progress in acquiring different skills. Parents were supposed to make sure children followed the prescribed path, and were allowed to follow their curiosity. This meant that parents were mainly observers of their children's maturation. Schools were there to give children the structures that they needed to learn efficiently. And children were meant to mature on their own—learning to be modern agents of their own lives.

ANIMALS AND MONSTERS

Because growing up is supposed to be natural, children are not taught by parents and teachers how to act appropriately within the culture of childhood. So, children turn to the books, toys, films, and cartoons addressed to them to try to understand the culture they are expected to inhabit. By seeing children depicted in media as animals and monsters—natural creatures with a wild side—they have a way to understand why they are sometimes treated as disruptive monsters and other times sheltered as too innocent (like a pet) to safely navigate adult society. And seeing adults pictured in stories as either virtuous caregivers or evil predators like ogres and witches, children learn to attach to parents and be wary of others, particularly strangers.

Children's media teases out some of the cultural and moral dynamics in conceptions of childhood hidden behind developmental models, making visible cultural imaginaries of the child, but also locating children in stages of development. Dr. Seuss's *Cat in the Hat*,[20] for example, illustrates the view of children as prone to the devil, but also suggests school-age children can manage disruptive feelings through imaginative play.

As the book begins, a school-age brother and sister are sitting at home alone, trying to be good, when a devilish alter ego in the form of a large cat in a hat arrives at the door. The Cat in the Hat is both animal and monster, an inner impulse or benign devil, encouraging the kids to have fun by playing havoc. The cat shows the kids how to dream up wild activities, and although at first they are wary, they love it. But they also urge the Cat in the Hat to leave, treating him as a transient impulse. There is no trace of the cat when the parents come home because these children have learned to cause havoc only in their imagination.[21]

---

[19] Nicholas Sammond, *Babes in Tomorrowland: Walt Disney and the Making of the American Child, 1930–1960* (Durham: Duke University Press, 2005), chapter 5.

[20] Theodore Geisel (Dr. Seuss), *Cat in the Hat* (New York: Random House, 1957).

[21] L. S. Vygotsky, *Mind in Society: The Development of Higher Psychological Processes*, ed. Michael Cole (Cambridge, MA: Harvard University Press, 1980).

The greater susceptibility of younger children to devilish impulses is presented in Maurice Sendak's book, *Where the Wild Things Are*.[22] The hero, Max, is a pre-school aged boy who gets angry and has a temper tantrum, so he is sent to bed without his supper. As he gets angrier, he sees himself as a monster, and sails away to where the "wild things are" to join the other monsters. He enjoys the freedom of doing terrible things and gnashing his terrible teeth with the monsters, but after a while, he wants to go home. His temper tantrum over, he wants his dinner. His bad behavior is real, but transitory—just part of growing up.

Enlightenment ideas about children as natural learners and pet-like charmers dominate children's media in the US because these are the liberal views of children that permeate schools and parenting magazines. Figures like Kermit the Frog (see Figure 7.10) and Miss Piggy from *The Muppets* are perfect representations of Enlightenment childhood. They are complementary in their gender roles as well curious innocents with good hearts and abundant charm.

Kermit is the natural leader of the Muppets because of his good character and an inner moral compass; the others trust and rely on him to be sensible. Miss Piggy, on the other hand, is Rousseau's natural school-age girl—just as smart as Kermit but drawn away from rationality by her desire for Kermit's attention. In the world of the Muppets, however, the great divide lies not between genders but between children and adults. Grown-ups are a source of horrifying corruption: they eat frogs' legs, engage in fraud and crime, and are too foolish to know what is good for them. The Muppets know better and, like pets or stuffed animals, represent good nature.[23]

FIGURE 7.10 *Kermit the Frog*

Many of the fairy tales retold in children books, cartoons, and Disney features are from the Renaissance, and describe older children's with school-age competencies. Many are still represented as animals and face corrupt adults, but they are more crafty in the ways they triumph over evil figures. "Puss in Boots," for example, helps his master, the son of a miller, to take over an ogre's palace and marry a princess, simply using his natural wits and wiles. This story helps to flesh out Renaissance ideas about children as just illiterate, not incompetent. But Puss in Boots remade by Disney is presented as a school-age prankster capable of using imaginative skills to overturn evil.[24]

---

[22] Maurice Sendak, *Where the Wild Things Are* (New York: Harper and Row, 1963).

[23] *The Muppet Show* (Jim Henson, 1976–81); *The Muppet Movie* (Jim Henson, 1979).

[24] *Puss in Boots* (Walt Disney, 1922).

FIGURE 7.11 *Little Red Riding Hood Meeting the Wolf.* The Traditional Faery Tales of Little Red Riding Hood

The stories of *Hansel and Gretel* and *Little Red Riding Hood* tell of childhood innocence and vulnerability in which children who are not animals are threatened by adults who are the animals or monsters. The first describes a witch who tries to lure a brother and sister into her house with gingerbread treats. She offers them things to eat because she wants to eat them. Their desires are much less dangerous than hers. Similarly, the wolf in *Little Red Riding Hood* (see Figure 7.11) uses charm to try to tempt Little Red Riding Hood away from her duty to her grandmother. This failing, he dresses up like the grandmother. But the true innocent can still tell the difference between a good granny and a bad wolf.

The wolf and the witch attract children with the corrupting tools of society: delicious treats, deceptive costuming, courtly manners, and powers that seem magical. But the children prevail because they are naturally good.

Fairy tales like these help provide children with some insight into the cultural complexity of the tradition of modern childhood, introducing them to a culture they are expected to navigate on their own.[25] Even sanitized Disney versions point to this cultural richness, while trying to reconcile old stories with developmental themes. As Sammond[26] has argued, Disney became a proponent of developmental theories of childhood, and used this model to make his films family friendly. Parents who learned about developmental childhood could see it mirrored in Disney films. At the same time, in retelling fairy tales, Disney provided children with a way of gaining access to the complex cultural genealogy of childhood, learning about the dreams and nightmares about children that lay behind scientific tales of maturation.

THE PROBLEM OF MODERN SELVES

Childhood is in principle egalitarian, but as Annette Lareau and Kristin Luker have shown,[27] children from different races and classes have ended up inhabiting different cultures of childhood. Poor families have been much more concerned about moral discipline

---

[25] Chandra Mukerji and Tarleton Gillespie, "Recognizable Ambiguity: Cartoon Imagery and American Childhood in Animaniacs," in Dan Cook (ed.), *Symbolic Childhood* (New York: Peter Lang Publishers, 2002), pp. 227–54.

[26] Sammond, *Babes in Tomorrowland.*

[27] Annette Lareau, *Unequal Childhoods: Class, Race, and Family Life* (Berkeley and Los Angeles: University of California Press, 2011); Kristin Luker, *When Sex Goes to School* (New York: W.W. Norton, 2006).

and danger for children, maintaining Protestant traditions of child-rearing. Middle-class parents emphasize Enlightenment ideas of natural curiosity and rationality, and offer their children more opportunities at home to make choices like citizens. So, even if parents of all classes identify children as potentially innocent and vulnerable and want them to get an education, their understanding of how to raise them can vary enormously.

Schools expect children to be natural learners in the Enlightenment tradition—whether they have been raised in that culture or not. As Christo Sims[28] has demonstrated, this misconception routinely leads to failures for children and teachers trying to ameliorate class inequality by freeing up children in classrooms. For children raised according to Protestant values, more freedom in the classroom is just confusing, not helpful. Naturalizing childhood, obscuring the different traditions that still are important to the behavior of parents, has made it harder for teachers and parents to share common goals, and develop teaching methods designed to fit different family cultures. The result is unequal childhoods and educational outcomes. But because childhood has been naturalized, the failures of children in educational experiments are taken as their own fault even when the ability to succeed is biased by class cultures of childhood.

In this way, developmental models that naturalize childhood end up reproducing differences that have cultural foundations. By junior high or high school, students belong to racial, class, and gender peer groups that map onto differences in the adult world. White middle-class practices of child development define what is more civilized. Groups of students are ranked no longer by age but in terms of the geopolitical conceptions of difference. Natural childhood reproduces the ranks it is expected to erase. Still, childhood remains the one discursive category of modern social types that has been successfully naturalized. It makes modern conceptions of rationality and personal agency the purpose of schooling, and also denies that the civilizing process in developmental childhood is political by defining child development as natural.

---

[28] Christo Sims, *The Cutting Edge of Fun* (Princeton: Princeton University Press, forthcoming); Sims, "From Differentiated Use to Differentiating Practices," *Information, Communication and Society* (2014), 17(6): 670–82.

PART THREE

POPULAR TOOLS OF MODERN LIFE

CHAPTER EIGHT

DIGITAL GAMES AND NAVIGATING MODERNITY

Modernity may be formally described as natural and progressive, but it is not always easy to navigate or understand. It is hard to know what to do when you have freedom of choice, and harder to accept a lack of freedom when the opposite seems promised. It is easy to feel alone in a culture that emphasizes individual action and sets you within communities of strangers. It is also hard to feel content when your standing depends on your latest achievements, and yet your ability to do anything is circumscribed by shifting circumstances. It is difficult, too, to learn how to become a modern adult starting as a child to whom adults are identified as dangerous strangers. And it is worse if you are categorized as a degraded social type yourself, identified as unworthy by nature. These discomforts are detritus from the articulation of modern principles and the powerful idea of progress that began in the 18th to 19th centuries. They make living in modern worlds confusing and anxious. They impel people toward forms of culture that address their anxieties, and give them a chance to play with or laugh at the routine tyrannies and cultural contradictions of modern life. If groups cannot avoid modern culture, they can take hold of it and make light of its principles in virtual worlds.

Modern media—from film to Facebook—are used for these purposes. They not only represent modernity, but also embody its principles in their technology. They both enact and defamiliarize taken-for-granted aspects of modern culture, making them available for practicing cultural skills and reflecting on common-sense practices.[1]

Digital games are an example. They are built with simulation technology from the military, and provide environments in which players can practice exercising agency in a structured environment, working toward goals and measuring their advancement and

---

[1] George Lipsitz, *Time Passages: Collective Memory and American Popular Culture* (University of Minnesota Press, 1990); Chris Rojek, *The Labour of Leisure: The Culture of Free Time* (London: Sage, 2010).

levels of competence. They are games of self-improvement for self-fashioning individuals, learning from experience[2] while meeting standards set by others.

I want to focus in this chapter on digital maze games, or games that use maze structures to organize the form of digital play. A "maze game" is not a genre category that is widely used in the game industry because it does not describe either the experience of play or subject matter of the game. Rather it describes the architecture of games that is often invisible to players. Gazzard[3] suggests up to half of arcade games use maze architecture, and maze structures are used widely on many platforms. Such games are fun to play, Gazzard argues, because of the challenge of negotiating complex spaces in trying to achieve a goal. Digital maze games have paths that are hard to navigate to find ways forward. So, players learn to negotiate a world they do not control and cannot fully understand.

Some games are simple and have obvious mazes like *Pac-Man*, while others like *Doom* have complex walls, doors, false paths, pools, fires, and hidden passageways. Some are adventure games that come with maps to help players find a way to achieve a goal. Many do not present themselves as mazes at all, but still use maze architecture to make players think strategically about how to go forward. Games of all sorts—from *Super Mario Brothers* to *Spider-Man 2 (3D)*—use paths to direct play, taking avatars through sewer systems, architectural complexes, or meandering alleys, paths, and streets to confront and outwit enemies. The point is to dominate the landscape, but doing so well requires learning the intricacies of the environment. In these spaces, avatars repeatedly die, requiring players to reassert their alter egos and start play again—like good neoliberal moderns inhabiting a risk economy.[4] Gamers who master skills of play take control of their destinies, working with imperfect information and reaching unfamiliar levels in the games. Each time they succeed in one set of tasks, they are faced with new problems to master. In this sense, they experience themselves as historical actors, facing shifting circumstances,[5] but they also learn how to act as free agents in a rigged game.

Playing games is challenging, but also comforting as a way to escape normal social life, and to enter a safe backstage for rehearsing skills of modern adulthood. Youth in particular are vulnerable creatures and often find life confusing, so public displays of cultural incompetence can be frequent, personally painful, and socially awkward. Practicing skills in games keeps the instruction more private. In virtual worlds of fictional play, winning and losing can have limited social consequences. And as long as games are defined as silly or funny—outside real life—they can serve as powerful rehearsal spaces or backstages for preparing for more serious performances of self.[6]

---

[2] Brian Sutton-Smith, *The Ambiguity of Play* (Cambridge, MA: Harvard University Press, 1997).

[3] Alison Gazzard, *Mazes in Videogames: Meaning, Metaphor and Design* (Jefferson, NC and London: McFarland & Company, Inc., 2013), particularly chapter 1; Eiko Ikegami, "Visualizing the Networked Self: Agency, Reflexivity and the Social Life of Avatars," *Social Research* (2011), 78(4): 1155–84.

[4] Gina Neff, *Venture Labor: Work and the Burden of Risk in Innovative Industries* (Cambridge, MA: MIT Press, 2012).

[5] Gazzard, *Mazes in Videogames*, chapter 5.

[6] Erving Goffman, *Presentation of Self in Everyday Life* (Garden City, NY: Doubleday Anchor, 1959).

Digital maze games designed for older school children or young adults often address disquieting, dangerous, or seductive aspects of modern culture like power, money, intolerance, greed, and sexuality. Navigating the mazes is hard, and full of dangers and surprises hidden around corners. Players fight to stay alive in extreme versions of dangerous adulthood. In many games, players enact heroic stories of individual achievement and moral courage. With sophisticated games using cutting-edge technology, players vicariously engage with the changing digital world, too, learning lessons in how to work with machines. These are all serious aspects of modernity embedded in digital maze games that players learn about as they seek paths through the mazes.

In this chapter, I will analyze digital maze games partly by exploring the concept of serious games, and partly by contextualizing them in the history of mazes. They are serious games in part because they have technological roots in military simulations. They are also serious because they engage players in consequential games of modern self-making. At the same time, digital maze games have roots in earlier mazes used for describing life paths and ways of negotiating them. Mazes have traditionally symbolized powers beyond the control of those who traverse them, requiring individuals to obey constraints they cannot change. Digital maze games call up these traditions, echoing the struggle of generations to think self-consciously about life paths, but focusing on problems of modern agency that put the culture in play.

GAMES AS PEDAGOGICAL TOOLS

As Huizinga argues, when people play a game, they practice the rules of the game; so to the extent the rules embody important cultural stakes, the game teaches players skills in navigating that culture. In terms from Alfred Schutz,[7] game worlds are non-ordinary realities in which people practice skills of everyday competence. He argues that daily life takes place in ordinary reality—the realm of normal experience that people take to be real or true. Media like films, novels, games, and comedy routines present non-ordinary realities or parallel worlds. These alternate realities are distinct from the everyday world of political and economic life, but they engage with exactly the same cultural principles and imaginaries that shape political and economic activity. Non-ordinary realities just embed taken-for-granted culture in virtual worlds where people can play with it in safety.[8] For young players, many games offer them a chance to enter virtual worlds of adulthood and try out activities denied to them in everyday life.[9] Players destroy evil, they save the world, they acquire special powers, but most of all, they try to improve their ability to make a life for themselves.

---

[7] Alfred Schutz, *The Phenomenology of the Social World* (Evanston, IL: Northwestern University Press, 1970).

[8] Gazzard, *Mazes in Videogames*, chapter 4.

[9] L. S. Vygotsky, *Mind in Society: The Development of Higher Psychological Processes*, ed. Michael Cole (Cambridge, MA: Harvard University Press, 1980); Dorothy Holland, William S. Lachicotte, Jr., Debra Skinner, and Carole Cain, *Identity and Agency in Cultural Worlds* (Cambridge, MA: Harvard University, 1998).

Contemporary digital games are mainly marketed to kids even though the games are also played by adults. Some war games like *World of Tanks* require so much technical knowledge of weapons and vehicles that they seem designed for former or active-duty soldiers more than kids. But many more digital games are based on traditional kids' activities, such as selling lemonade, delivering newspapers, or collecting pretty things from nature. They are designed to teach children skills appropriate to each stage of development, practicing skills of their culture by working with rules of the game.

Games also use jokes and the carnivalesque[10] to make themselves transgressive and funny. They ridicule and distort serious cultural issues, putting fingers in the holes and folds of the cultural fabric to reveal its weaknesses. Their breaches of decorum make these virtual worlds irreverent and fascinating. They face down the terror of modernity, embracing unknown futures and flaunting their untested selves. Cartoonish or ghoulish characters in dystopian settings make the ailments of modernity seem worse, but also a challenge to innocence. Rather than being reassuring, these games are provocative, making fearful enemies seem so awful and absurd that players can both fear and laugh out loud at them.

As Mary Douglas[11] has argued, jokes are funny because they point to contradictions in a culture. Laughing expresses discomfort with these lapses and folds, and turns them into pleasure. Games often reveal these weaknesses by reversals of cultural values—as in Carnival—making conventional conceptions of virtue the butt of jokes. Laughter and contempt make the wounds of everyday modern life more tolerable. They make clear that something is wrong without having to articulate what it is. Jokes about gender and race, for example, ease the pain of discrimination, and comedy routines about politics make light of the fact that modern citizens have little power. Similarly, digital games addressed to young people that have carnivalesque elements ridicule the adult world, making the hardships of becoming modern adults amusing.

SERIOUS GAMES OF MILITARY SIMULATION

Digital maze games are "serious" in two distinct ways, one of which is military. The term "serious games" is most commonly used to describe the simulations of nuclear war used in the Cold War. These provided the technological foundations for contemporary digital games. The Cold War simulations are in turn part of a long tradition of military games—a history of war games transforming bloody struggles of life and death into safe games of strategy. Games of virtual combat date back all the way to the ancient world, starting with chess in ancient India and tabletop simulations of war in Ancient Greece.[12] Chess was elaborated over time,

---

[10] Mikhail Bakhtin, *Rabelais and His World* (Bloomington: Indiana University Press, 1984).

[11] Mary Douglas, "Jokes," in Chandra Mukerji and Michael Schudson (eds), *Rethinking Popular Culture* (Berkeley and Los Angeles: University of California Press, 1991), pp. 291–310.

[12] Roger D. Smith, *Military Simulations and Serious Games* (Oviedo, FL: Modelbenders, 2009).

and so were tabletop games of war. Modeling battlements, for example, became a popular preoccupation for gentlemen during the period of siege warfare in Europe (See Figure 8.1).

Such simulations became more serious tools of military planning in the late 17th century, when the military engineer Sébastien Le Prestre de Vauban had miniature fortresses and cities built for Louis XIV based on exact measurements.[13] War for Vauban (and other military engineers in this period) required both battlefield strategies and architectural knowledge to lay out or undermine defenses effectively.[14] His "plans-relief" emphasized the strengths and weaknesses of fortifications, and allowed him to demonstrate to the king how to use troops to attack or defend places.[15]

Jousts and mock battles were also court entertainments that simulated armed confrontations, and exercised military skills. Noble families descended from knights could display their skills as warriors or the abilities of those that served them, making these mock battles serious games of power.

Making models and simulating battles at home became popular with the middle class in the 18th and 19th centuries, using toy soldiers and model defenses. These games were played by both children and adults. For boys, these were serious games of gender formation, and for middle-class men, they provided a chance to acquire strategic and logistical skills vicariously.

Digital simulations of warfare became possible in the 20th century with the rise of game theory after WWII. Game theory was a mathematical way of modeling patterns of cooperation and conflict, looking at the probabilities of outcomes to different kinds of encounters. Zero sum games of probability were good for modeling the struggle between the US and the Soviet Union in which success for one side was failure for the other. So, during the Cold War, simulation was used to imagine nuclear war and its consequences short of setting off bombs.[16] This allowed modern states

FIGURE 8.1 *Making Military Models for Simulating Battles. Sébastien le Clerc, 17th Century*

---

[13] George A. Rothrock, "The Musée des Plans-Reliefs," *French Historical Studies* (1969), 6(2): 253–6.

[14] For a longer discussion of strategics and logistics, see Chandra Mukerji, "The Territorial State as a Figured World of Power: Strategics, Logistics and Impersonal Rule," *Sociological Theory* (2010), 28(4): 402–25.

[15] Janis Langins, *Conserving the Enlightenment* (Cambridge, MA: MIT Press, 2004).

[16] Marc Prensky, "True Believers: Digital Game-Based Learning in the Military," in Prensky, *Digital Game-Based Learning* (New York: McGraw-Hill, 2001); Paul Edwards, *The Closed World: Computers and the Politics of Discourse in Cold War America* (Cambridge, MA: MIT Press, 1996).

FIGURE 8.2 *Flight Simulator*

to think about their history and destiny through games of probability and chance.

The military also developed flight simulators after WWII to teach recruits how to use complicated and expensive weapons systems without putting themselves or the machinery at risk (see Figure 8.2). More realistic simulators did a better job of training, so the military pushed for higher representational accuracy and better graphics. More realistic play was also more engaging so the simulations that had been made more exact for practical reasons also became more fun to play.

Playing war in digital formats was entertaining enough to encourage the military to develop games to attract young people to the armed services (see Figure 8.3). At the same time, the military continued to fund new kinds of simulations for strategic use. On-screen simulations made drone warfare possible, turning lethal battles into things on the screen. And the military funded the development of treatments for

FIGURE 8.3 *War Simulation Games in Military Training. Soldiers from the Royal Artillery in Simulation Tent*

soldiers with PTSD that addressed traumatic memories with war scenarios. Digital games were made serious tools of modern war and military culture.[17]

Commercial game designers repurposed military technology for profit. Combat games were early successes because boys still wanted to learn to fight, if only vicariously. Playing at being warriors turned interest in violence into imaginative play.[18] Commercial companies also diversified the types of games, digitizing popular games of adventure and quests. In this way, they turned serious games of war into virtual worlds of play for the next generation.[19]

MAZES AND SERIOUS GAMES OF LIFE

The term "serious game" is also used in anthropology to describe practices of negotiating the problematic contours of power in everyday life.[20] This kind of serious play can be addressed virtually with mazes, including digital maze games. Mazes provide paths for people to walk that are structured by a power beyond their control—a form of order imposed on them. In this sense, mazes are serious games of power and agency. Mazes treat human existence as an unfolding, embodied experience that is governed by forces beyond clear comprehension. The paths are both ways through virtual worlds, and places distinct from life. In this sense, they are serious games about power and personal existence, addressing the deeply human problem of managing the twists and turns of experiences beyond their control, and determining what to do next.

Historically, most of what we call mazes have been unicursal, meaning there is only one route through them. The route is so complex that even when people see the maze as a whole, they are not able to anticipate the path completely. In this type of maze, life has a true path that lies beyond human comprehension, and people must practice staying on the path in spite of their doubts about where they are going.

Mazes found in rock art and ancient turf mazes are unicursal. Scandinavian turf mazes, the most common ancient mazes, are thought to be paths between human and spirit worlds. They are seen as liminal sites in which evil spirits as well as good forces can travel. Sailors, for this reason, are said to have walked these mazes before going to sea to trap demons that might imperil their journey.[21]

---

[17] Marisa Brandt, *War, Trauma and Technologies of the Self: Making of Virtual Reality Exposure Therapy* (Dissertation, University of California, San Diego, 2013); Tim Lenoir and Henry Lowood, "Theaters of War: The Military-Entertainment Complex," http://web.stanford.edu/class/sts145/Library/Lenoir-Lowood_TheatersOfWar.pdf

[18] D. Michael and S. Chen, *Serious Games* (Boston, MA: Thompson Course Technology, 2006).

[19] Sherry Ortner, *Anthropology and Social Theory: Culture, Power, and the Acting Subject* (Durham and London: Duke University Press, 2006).

[20] Ortner, *Anthropology and Social Theory*, chapter 6.

[21] David Willis McCullough, *The Unending Mystery* (New York: Random House, 2004), chapters 1 and 5.

FIGURE 8.4 *Saffron Walden Turf Maze*

There remain turf mazes in Britain similar to their Scandinavian counterparts, one example being the maze at Saffron Walden (see Figure 8.4). It is either an ancient turf maze or an imitation of one. We only know that it was rebuilt in the 17th century.[22] The Saffron Walden maze is set on a village green, and lies in a region where other village greens have mazes, too. The one at Saffron Walden is just a particularly large and complex geometrical structure, and has a topographical complexity that is interesting.

The Saffron Walden maze is composed of recessed paths and raised berms of turf. The path is dirt, now reinforced with bricks. The structure is so large that it takes more than half an hour to walk through it. It is captivating in a physical sense because once you are in it, you are there for a long time. There is no way out except to complete the journey or reject the path. The maze's twists and turns create an immersive experience.

Although there is no way to go wrong in following a unicursal maze, it is hard to predict where the path will go next. The maze at Saffron Walden starts with twists and turns that seem to move toward the center of the maze—the goal of the journey—but the path soon veers farther and farther from the center, finally looping around the outer corners of the maze. The maze has four quadrants, but the path does not go systematically through them in order. The path often stays in a quadrant for a while, looping back at grassy berms that rise up between the quadrants. But periodically, the path pierces the barrier, moving into a different quadrant and even to the other side of the maze. Following the path is active work, and the maze's geometry becomes an experience of motion. Whether or not this turf maze has sacred significance or stands for something else, following the long path certainly feels like ritual movement, the geometry acting as a higher order that humans enter without fully comprehending what they are doing or where they are going.[23]

The most famous maze from the ancient world was the Labyrinth of Knossos. According to Ovid, the labyrinth was built on Crete for King Minos to capture the Minotaur—a monstrous half bull, half man produced by Minos' wife after copulation with a bull. Minos asked Daedalus, an architect, to create a maze to hold the Minotaur, so Daedalus made the labyrinth of Knossos so confusing that even he had trouble exiting it; it was both a puzzle and a cage, linking worlds but also keeping them apart.[24]

---

[22] Gazzard, *Mazes in Videogames*, chapter 2.

[23] Gazzard, *Mazes in Videogames*, chapter 2.

[24] McCullough, *The Unending Mystery*, chapter 2.

Minos used the Minotaur and maze to avenge the death of his son by the Athenians. The king demanded that seven young men and seven young women from Athens be sacrificed every seven years to the Minotaur. Once sent into the labyrinth, they could not find their way out, but the Minotaur would find them. Theseus, the son of the sea god, Poseidon, was horrified by the sacrifice, and vowed to enter the labyrinth to kill the Minotaur. It was his quest—a way to acquire the renown appropriate to a man of his parentage.[25]

The first two groups of Athenian youths demanded by Minos were lost to the Minotaur, but Theseus joined the third group and entered the labyrinth undetected with his sword. Ariadne, the daughter of Minos, had fallen in love with the young and handsome hero, and asked Daedalus for help to find a way for Theseus to escape. On the architect's advice, she gave Theseus a thread to unroll as he walked into the labyrinth that he later could follow out. With her help, Theseus killed the Minotaur, freed the Athenians, and emerged from the labyrinth. He escaped with Ariadne, but then deserted her on an island, returning to Athens on his own to become its ruler. He was considered weak for instituting democracy, but in the end, Theseus became a hero for seeking good more than power.[26]

The story of Theseus and the Minotaur became widely popular in Rome as well as Greece, and images of the man and beast engaged in battle became common on pottery, walls, and above all, the floors of houses. There is an example of a Roman floor maze in Figure 8.5. It illustrates how the idea of the maze was adapted to Roman culture. As would be expected, Theseus is in the middle of this maze, fighting the Minotaur. But the structure around him is depicted as less a maze than architecture. This way of depicting the myth frequently appeared on the floors of grand houses on newly acquired Roman territory, and it made particular sense there. Roman conquerors clearly had reason to celebrate the warrior virtues in Theseus, but they also had a motive for celebrating Daedalus the architect. The Romans used engineering to develop, connect, and protect their colonies, so building was intrinsic to exercising power within the Empire.

More complex unicursal mazes were found on the floors of Gothic Cathedrals. These were ritual sites walked by believers to gain spiritual awareness. The repetition in walking the maze was a way to learn kinesthetically the presence of a higher power. The fact that the paths were unicursal conveyed that there was only one true path for good Christians to follow—the one designed by God. And the geometry

FIGURE 8.5 *Theseus and Minotaur in Center of a Roman Mosaic Maze*

---

[25] McCullough, *The Unending Mystery*, chapter 2.
[26] McCullough, *The Unending Mystery*, chapter 2.

FIGURE 8.6 *Amiens Cathedral Maze*

demonstrated in its complexity and geometrical perfection both the beauty of God's plan and its incomprehensibility to ordinary people.[27]

The maze in the Amiens Cathedral (see Figure 8.6) is an example. The Amiens Cathedral was an important pilgrimage site because it housed what was purported to be the head of John the Baptist. The pilgrims, coming to the church to pay their respects to this relic and saint, would also walk the maze. They followed the dark line through the octagonal figure, encouraged by the maze's twists and turns to contemplate the spiritual significance of directions in Christian iconography—particularly the East as the site of the resurrection.[28] The point of the practice was not only personal experience of the divine order, but also, as Gazzard[29] notes, the creation of a Christian community around ritual practices of pilgrimage.

Walking the maze was an act of obedience to the church as well as God. The design at the center of the maze stood for the triumph of the Church. Portraits of four men were

---

[27] McCullough, *The Unending Mystery*, chapter 4; Gazzard, *Mazes in Videogames*, chapter 4.

[28] Amelia Carolina Sparavigna, "Ad Orientem: The Orientation of Gothic Cathedrals of France," http://arxiv. org/pdf/1209.2338.pdf

[29] Gazzard, *Mazes in Videogames*, chapter 4.

FIGURE 8.7 *Villa Pisani Maze*

separated by a set of crossed batons that in the Roman tradition represented institutional power. The men were originally Bishop Evrard, who first commissioned the church, the king reigning at that time, Louis, and two architects or masons who built it: Master Luzarches Robert and Master Thomas de Cormont. (After the Revolution, the king was replaced by Cormont's son, Renault.)[30] The figures were surrounded by angels, suggesting that by building the cathedral and supporting the Church, they served the will of God.

Starting in the Renaissance, mazes were set in gardens of the rich and powerful, and began to be multicursal or have multiple paths, some with dead ends. Questions of obedience to higher powers and individual agency were secularized and reconfigured. Now, getting out of these mazes became the challenge. The garden mazes had high hedges, providing little information for those trying to traverse them. But visitors still had to make choices—many of which would be wrong—and bear the consequences of their mistakes. So, those navigating Renaissance garden mazes exercised free will, but within a game of power set by landholders.

A good example of a garden maze of this sort is in the garden of the Villa Pisani near Venice (see Figure 8.7). The tight geometrical figure of the maze is organized around a central viewing platform on which visitors can see the maze as a whole, and laugh at those who are lost in it. Seen from above, the maze is clearly a model of land control—the exercise of power through property. The maze is also a test of individual ingenuity. Because it

---

[30] www.luc.edu/medieval/labyrinths/amiens.shtml

PLAN DV
LABIRINTHE
DE VERSAILLES.

FIGURE 8.8 *Plan of the Labyrinthe of Versailles*

is multicursal, it challenges people to learn the secrets of the geometry, and find a path out of it.[31]

The *Labyrinthe* of Versailles[32] (see Figure 8.8) was less geometrically complex, but also had false paths to trick visitors and demonstrate their subordination to the king's power. But it had in addition a set of fountains based on Aesop's Fables, teaching lessons in self-governance. The entrance to the labyrinth was flanked by sculptures of Aesop and Cupid, presenting alternative guides to the labyrinth of life. Cupid stood for the thread of love that one could follow through one's mortal journey, and Aesop stood for the thread of wisdom.[33]

The small fountains based on Aesop's Fables were charming landmarks that helped people negotiate the maze, but they also conveyed lessons about life derived from the ancients. The fountain of the owl and the birds, for example, showed the danger of not listening to those with wisdom. The wise owl stopped talking to the silly birds who ignored him, keeping his own counsel. The fountain of the fox and stork taught that cheating was self-defeating. The fox offered the stork dinner in a shallow plate, putting the food where the stork could not reach it. In return the stork offered the fox dinner in a long-necked container too narrow for the fox's nose. These fountains and their counterparts provided lessons in self-governance for modern selves, using stories from classical culture that taught virtues required for French court life.[34]

All of the mazes from prehistoric times to the modern world consisted of pathways through systems of constraint. The difficulty of traversing mazes made them sites for thinking about the problem of knowing how to live. Unicursal mazes defined a true path, while multicursal mazes provided choices that could be wrong, playing with issues of self-governance. Walking either kind of maze was a "serious game" in Ortner's[35] sense, confronting people with landscapes of power to negotiate. They provided visceral, experiential means of learning what it meant to find a path in life in a world beyond one's control.

---

[31] McCullough, *The Unending Mystery*, chapter 6.

[32] I will not draw a distinction between mazes and labyrinths in this chapter because it is not relevant to the analysis, and confusing across languages since the labyrinth at Versailles was a maze.

[33] Charles Perrault, Sébastien Le Clerc, and Michel Conan, *Le Labyrinthe de Versailles 1677* (Paris: Editions du Moniteur, 1982).

[34] Perrault et al., *Le Labyrinthe de Versailles 1677*.

[35] Ortner, *Anthropology and Social Theory*.

DIGITAL MAZE GAMES AND MODERN SUBJECTIVITY

Contemporary digital games that use mazes as backbones are serious games for rehearsing modern personhood, offering paths to try and choices to make that are tactical. Contemporary maze games are passionate (even obsessive) objects of attention because they foreground problems of power and agency that plague modern people, particularly young people.[36] Unlike earlier mazes, the maze structure in digital games is often hidden, obscuring the playing field of power in the games. The avatars in digital games also die, requiring players to reinvent themselves and display personal commitment to a difficult task. Perhaps most importantly, in most digital games, there is no way out of the maze, making play more cyclical than progressive. In this way, modern digital games convey a false sense of freedom, teach a neoliberal practice of cyclical risk-taking, and provide practice in living in a system of power from which there is no escape, just a continuous struggle to go on.

Some maze-like games are easy to recognize as mazes, one example being *PacMan*. Simple avatars move in a quasi-maze space, and are threatened by silly ghosts. There is no single path to follow and many ways to go, but ghosts keep blocking some openings, so players are faced with limited choices of where to go, quickly strategizing the best route forward. *PacMan* is like a tabletop war game but without clear winners or losers. Success is less like winning a battle than reaching a new grade in school. The game teaches players to improve their abilities through practice—fundamental skills for modern selves living in a culture that values progress.

Adventure games with maze structures seem more like stories, focusing on the path more than structures of constraint. Mixing together bits and pieces of history and mythology, tests of heroism are merged with coming-of-age stories. Young heroes advance to gain a place in the world. Many of these games explore spiritual themes and moral threats. Evil is embodied in monsters or corrupt adults who are defeated by the innocent but virtuous young. The games vary in what they emphasize about modern life, and the personal qualities of individuals that are most valued. But they all make game play a journey. They test the strategic and tactical competencies of players by the way they structure the paths and barriers of virtual worlds.

MAGE AND MINIONS

Mage and Minions for the iPad is visually a tabletop war game, and narratively defined as a quest, but it emphasizes the control of assets as key to logistical power. It is a hack and slash game with lots of blood, but the fighting is not very realistic because the graphics are

---

[36] For passion and attachment to objects of culture, see Antoine Hennion and J.-M. Fouquet, *Grandeur de Bach: L'Amour de la Musique en France au XIXe Siècle* (Paris: Fayard, 2000), and Claude Benzecry, *The Opera Fanatic* (Chicago: University of Chicago Press, 2011).

not sophisticated. The game shows the action from a bird's-eye point of view, so the player can see enemies coming before the avatars do, and like a general, prepare for battle. This is the time to choose assets from the inventory appropriate to the threat. During battles, too, the player can use the touch screen to circle targets, and call up weapons. Skill in the game requires balancing action with inventory. *Mage and Minions* is clearly a descendent of military simulations, but it also teaches liberal values by making success in war contingent on managing property.

The cinematic introduction for *Mage and Minions* makes the dual character of the game clear by posing the following questions: Is this a quest for restoring the moral order? Or is it an opportunity to take gold from the dead? The answer seems to be both. The world of *Mage and Minions* is presented as medieval, but this historical conceit just makes the game carnivalesque. Elements of the modern world are simply labeled with terms from other worlds. The enemies are evil spirits or ogres. Avatars collect "treasure." And players make new weapons and armor by "crafting". Still, playing *Mage and Minions* is serious training in liberal capitalism and modern military strategy, using economic logics and logistical control of assets for strategic advantage. Players even have the option of paying money to have things crafted instead of doing it themselves. In this carnivalesque world, the medieval imagery and language deny the very modernity that players practice in the game.

SPIDER-MAN 2 (3D)

Spider-Man 2 (3D) uses high-resolution graphics to tell a coming-of-age story about Spider-Man. He becomes a good citizen in a corrupt world by staying apart from degenerate and evil adults. Peter Parker is the young man who becomes Spider-Man, and uses his superhero powers to save New York City from the chaos spawned by incompetent, greedy adults. Spider-Man, a classic comic book hero, is capable of facing down the monster of urban violence and despair. Like Theseus, he takes it upon himself to save citizens of his city, and uses his unique powers for good.

The path to personal success for the player entails fighting evil in a series of miniature quests for finding and defeating bad guys. Approaching enemies means negotiating mazes of sewers, construction sites, and broken-down buildings, ending with bloody battles requiring a high degree of technical and tactical skill. Peter Parker has a range of suits to put on that give the superhero different attributes, so he can struggle against multiple forms of evil. But Spider-Man has defining qualities, too. He can fly between the buildings of New York City above the street, using web shooters to attach himself to buildings, first on one side and then another, or to hang above a crime scene waiting for a strategic moment.

Technically, *Spider-Man 2 (3D)* uses sophisticated simulation software to depict New York architecture and neighborhoods realistically, and make the action convincing. The fast-moving pace and sophisticated graphics make the pursuit of bad guys dramatic, getting the superhero to where he can make a difference. He is an old comic book figure as are his archenemies, but the simulation technology makes fighting crime for Spider-Man and players a serious game of modern warfare. The sophistication of the game also poses challenges to players who can gain multiple, complex skills with practice. They not only engage enemies to establish competence, but also struggle against the software, too. So, they train themselves in skillful engagement with a digital world.

Peter Parker is a good citizen in Rousseau's sense with his own moral compass and capacity to act intelligently. When Spider-Man fights, however, he is noisy and profane, using his body and passions more than his rationality to prevail. Both Spider-Man and his opponents insult each other, spewing epithets, fat jokes, engaging in verbal bullying with their taunts. It is the kind of male adolescent banter that identifies Spider-Man as a young person in an adult world, baiting his enemies and trying to humiliate as well as destroy those who show him disrespect. But Spider-Man is also capable of beating adults because the most evil ones are portrayed as childlike, and he can rise above them (literally).

There is no clear path for Spider-Man to follow through this game because New York is not a single maze, but rather a set of them—neighborhoods with different characteristics beset by different crimes. There are a range of villains to counter and wrongs to right, too. At each level of play, the player can consult Spider-Man's smartphone and see on its map the crimes that Spider-Man can fight. The hero always finds a new wrong to right, inhabiting a corrupt world with no effective way out.

The cultural lesson is that corruption is endemic to modern (adult) life, and coming of age requires moral integrity and a willingness to fight for right. New York in this game has devolved into a Hobbesian state of nature, a war of all against all. Spider-Man defends modernity or the social contract against human weakness, running all the mazes in its defense. He fights for Western principles of progress against the corrupt adult world that has lost sight of these values or lost the courage to defend them.

FIGURE 8.9 *Escher Imagery, Orientalist Fantasy, and Ida's Quest of Repentance: Monument Valley (Screen Shot from Game)*

MONUMENT VALLEY

Monument Valley is a peaceful and beautiful maze game using sophisticated and counter-intuitive graphics as well as New Age music to tell a story of spiritual seeking and moral redemption (see Figure 8.9). The storyline is simple. A young princess, Ida, has stolen sacred objects, and in doing this, has destroyed a civilization. She is on a quest to redeem herself by restoring the crystals and jewels to their proper places. The path she needs to take for redemption goes through the same world she destroyed, so she must navigate broken bits of architecture. She seeks a route through dispersed pieces of houses and temples as they spin through the air or float on the sea. Ida cannot make the journey herself. The player must show her the path, discovering how to go by creating order out of chaos.

The beauty of the graphics and peaceful New Age music seem at odds with the post-apocalyptic storyline. But they underscore the spiritual rather than worldly character of Ida's journey. She wanders the world, seeking inner peace. She wants a unicursal path to redemption, but it is broken, so the player helps. Ida does not strategize like a modern individual, but leaves it to the player to help her, affirming the virtue of her quest.

Monument Valley teaches intuitive reasoning and draws attention to wonder and mystery as part of the maze tradition. It teaches the limits of self-interest (the shame of stealing beautiful things) and the importance of collective well-being (restoring social worlds). Princess Ida is mute, and can only move if the player taps the spot where she should go. Player and avatar have to form a team with different abilities to go anywhere. Players use touch to guide Ida's actions, but when Ida steps on important buttons, she also alters the world that they play in. Players can only help Ida by suspending belief in ordinary reality and intuitively solving the puzzles of the maze.

The civilization that Ida has ruined is vaguely Eastern or Oriental—distinguished from the modern West. She is not seeking modern qualities, but rather ones destroyed by the spread of modern values. The strange character of her quest is matched by the illogical visual relations in the game reminiscent of M. C. Escher drawings.[37] Ida can also walk as easily up the side of a building or upside down as she can walk on top of objects. In this virtual reality, normal relations do not hold either in gravity or geometry. That's the joke of the game. It plays with the limits of rationality as well as self-interest, and treats a cute little girl as the source of destruction of a great civilization. The post-apocalyptic world in which the game takes place is not grimy, dark, and ugly, either, but colorful and beautiful. The inversions locate Ida in a world of magical possibilities in which redemption is possible, and beauty of spirit matters. Still, players make progress to new levels of the game by using their intelligence to solve problems—as rational, modern selves.

Monument Valley emphasizes inarticulate modern practices, not modern principles. It teaches players to address the unexpected, and improvise new ways to get things done. It conveys the value of continual problem solving, and champions the possibility for individuals to reinvent themselves. Players are asked to think not just outside the box, but as though anything could be possible. Being mute, Ida places modernity outside discursive common sense, refusing Lockean individualism and Hobbes' state of nature.

---

[37] M. C. Escher, *M. C. Escher: The Graphic Work* (New York: Taschen America, 1992).

Princess Ida is a modern self who is holding herself responsible for her actions, and reforming her identity by her deeds. She has no enemies to defeat because she is her own worst enemy. She destroyed the world she now wants. She hopes to improve herself, not destroy others, and she understands what needs to be done. She runs into crows that inhibit her movements, but she does not hurt them. She finds an ally in a nonhuman agent: a pile of stones with an eye quite literally looking out for her. So, abandoning liberal ideals of property and progress, she sees that her happiness depends on the well-being of the world of humans and nonhumans as a whole.

GAMES OF MODERN LIFE

Each of these three games provides a model for surviving in the modern world. They emphasize different aspects of modernity but foreground skills required of modern individuals (adults). Players can take on the role of good citizens and pursue the collective good, they can engage in quests to eradicate threats to modern values, or they can pursue wealth and manage it to their advantage, or they can do good deeds to improve themselves. All the games engage with the problems of identity and agency, and address them in virtual worlds where players can make a joke or game of the difficulty of becoming modern selves.

Each game has its own view of modernity, and ideas about what is important for individuals to learn. *Monument Valley* emphasizes the importance of a personal moral compass in negotiating the complexity of life, and makes the pursuit of inner peace and collective happiness more important than liberal self-aggrandizement. *Spider-Man* focuses on the problem of becoming an adult in a modern world where adult corruption is everywhere and Hobbesian relations of nature dominate. Becoming a good person and responsible citizen is the job of those who can transcend the struggle, but requires young people who are willing to fight and face danger for the common good. *Mage and Minions* also teaches how to become a calculating modern liberal individual, managing money, inventory, and teams to wage wars and achieve goals. The point is to serve the forces of good rather than evil, but the medium for getting there is control of violence and wealth.

The games all tap into the maze tradition, organizing play around paths to new challenges and struggles. They engage with ideals of heroism, and are premised on the need for moral order. They all point to the military heritage of digital games, too, either engaging in simulated battles or looking at the destruction of civilization. And they engage players in the serious game of reflecting on their agency and structures of power. So entering these virtual worlds as avatars or agents, players can experience the thrill of being successful and reaching a new level of the game, proud of the abilities they have acquired to do so. But at the same time, they learn without noticing it to accommodate themselves to a modernity they cannot escape and that offers them repeated journeys along the same life path rather than real progress.

CHAPTER NINE

PHILOSOPHICAL MEDIA AND
CRITIQUES OF MODERNITY

Narrative media like film and television provide other cultural means for reflecting on modernity. They present "what if?" stories about how lives might be lived, raising questions about what it means to be a human being in the modern world. If digital games rehearse the skills of acting as a modern self, narrative media follow modern principles and practices through the passage of time. They look at modernity in motion and put conceptions of progress up for inspection. Rather than socializing players into modern roles and skills, these media serve as philosophical machinery for examining and questioning modernity. The technology stands apart from the human lives it portrays, questioning the gap between what is human and not human. The relentlessness of engineered motion, the indifference of patterns of light and dark on a screen, the appeal of material illusions, and the silence of the camera's eye all provide points of contrast to the stories of human life told in narrative media,[1] and opportunities for assessing modern culture against the machinery of the modern world.

In this chapter, I will analyze a set of films, looking at them as philosophical machinery, simulations of human lives that work as thought experiments. Thought experiments are hypotheticals, "what if?" stories that follow an idea or set of assumptions of a culture to the extreme, where their implications can be examined. Films often take human situations to an extreme to make the narratives dramatic or funny, so they provide the basis for thought experiments.

I take the term "philosophical machinery" from Jessica Riskin,[2] who describes the history of technology used to simulate the actions of people, animals, or spiritual figures in

---

[1]Gilles Deleuze, *Cinema 1: The Movement Image* (London: Athlone Press, 1986); Deleuze, *Cinema 2: The Time Image* (Minneapolis: University of Minnesota Press, 1989); Lesley Stern, *The Smoking Book* (Chicago: University of Chicago Press, 1999); Stern, *Dead and Alive* (Montreal: Caboose, 2012).
[2]Jessica Riskin, "The Defecating Duck, or the Ambiguous Origins of Artificial Life," *Critical Inquiry* (2003), 29: 599–633; Riskin, *Genesis Redux: Essays in the History and Philosophy of Artificial Life* (Chicago: University of Chicago Press, 2007).

FIGURE 9.1 *Vaucanson's Automata, including the Duck*

order to reflect on human character and conduct. Philosophical machines, Riskin writes, became particularly important in the 18th century when clockwork automata simulating animal or human behavior were used to test Cartesian ideas about the distinction between humans and animals. Artificial ducks and other figures were built to mimic the attributes of living creatures by technological means, defining human nature by what was missing in the machines (soul, free will) (see Figure 9.1).

The automata, philosophers argued, could act like animals, but could not engage in independent (moral) reasoning. Riskin described one famous automaton called the "Defecating Duck," which could act like an animal, eating and defecating, but could not engage in thought or exercise free will. The machine was used to describe human nature, distinguishing human agents from rule-following machines. Riskin contends that we still use modern media as philosophical machinery to consider what it means to be human.[3] She focuses on computers and artificial intelligence, arguing that the limits of digital technologies are now being taken as evidence of human superiority over machines.

I want to argue in this chapter that while films are not automata, they function as philosophical machinery in another sense. Films simulate human lives with machinery to consider what life has become in modern culture. Films depict the material unfolding of modern worlds, and organize stories around the passage of time and relations with things.[4] They both embody and hold up for examination principles of technological

---

[3] Riskin, *Genesis Redux.*

[4] This approach resembles the event analysis of Robin Wagner-Pacifici, following the unfolding of events. See Robin Wagner-Pacifici, "Theorizing the Restlessness of Events," *American Journal of Sociology* (2010), 115(5): 1351–86; Wagner-Pacifici, *The Art of Surrender* (Chicago: University of Chicago Press, 2005).

progress, and measures of improvement. And with its indifference, film highlights acts of deep humanity and their opposite, too.

Film as part of modern material culture also draws attention to things and their powers.[5] In theaters, objects glow in the light or hover as dark threats above the human action, inarticulate presences that provide evidence of how modernity works without making claims about what it is. The stories present hypothetical scenarios of what modern life might look like or what self-fashioning individuals might do, and the medium stands as witness to and measure of it.

To explore films as philosophical machinery, I will focus in this chapter on four very different examples: *No Country for Old Men* (Coen and Coen, 2007), *Einstein's Wife* (Woolmington, 2003), *Where the Heart Is* (Williams, 2000), and *Independence Day* (Emmerich, 1996). By posing "what if?" questions and depicting what could be or might be true, all of these films reveal and critique taken-for-granted assumptions about modern life. All use the indifference of the medium to depict unspeakable forces in ordinary lives. They show what cannot be said—cultural patterns too shocking or taken for granted to be easily discussed, and logics of power that depend for their efficacy on unconscious reproduction. They prod viewers to rethink common sense, consider what else might be true, and raise issues of moral and political philosophy that probe cultural silences.

Each film poses different questions about modern culture, but they all use the medium as a point of comparison for understanding the inner drives of characters, the power of modern discourse, the pursuit of material logics, and unspoken or unspeakable patterns of conduct. They bring to the screen the ghosts and shadows of modernity that often are obscured from view, and make them dramatic enough to see more clearly their inner workings.

NO COUNTRY FOR OLD MEN

The Coen brothers film, *No Country for Old Men* (Coen and Coen, 2007), is an Academy Award winning contemporary Western based on the book by Cormac McCarthy[6] set in the drug wars along the US–Mexican border. The story describes a Hobbesian world— one of continual warfare and uncertainty—produced by a sociopath. He shows a complete lack of compassion for others and no remorse for the pain they feel. *No Country for Old Men* is a thought experiment about individualism pushed to the extreme of sociopathology in an unfolding story of violence and cultural breakdown. In it, the camera—that rests on the faces of the confused victims that the sociopath does not care to see—comes to seem more human than the calculating killer.

---

[5] Stern, *The Smoking Book*; Stern, *Dead and Alive*.
[6] Cormac McCarthy, *No Country for Old Men* (New York: Vintage International, 2005).

No Country for Old Men was one of many films from 2007 addressing deep cultural anxieties about violence in American culture, including two others set in the American West: *3:10 to Yuma* (Mangold, 2007) and *There Will Be Blood* (Anderson, 2007). These three films portrayed horrifying worlds of violence and greed perpetrated by sociopaths, treating sociopathology as an extreme case of neoliberal individualism. The films were not political films about neoliberal bad actors like *Wolf of Wall Street* (Scorsese, 2013), but rather depicted the mythological American West in crisis, offering thought experiments about the modern world left in the hands of pathological individualists.

No Country for Old Men follows Anton Chigurh (Javier Bardem), a classical sociopath who is on a mission to recover drugs stolen from a drug cartel. He is driven by compulsion to kill anyone who gets in his way. He has little to say, and much to do. He is as soulless as Riskin's Defecating Duck, mechanically doing what he is programmed to do. He is clearly unnatural, but he is just as clearly a self-maximizing modern self, indifferent to those around him and determined to fulfill his contractual obligations.

FIGURE 9.2 *Chigurh and His Gun. The gun underscores his indifference to people, treating them simply as animals for slaughter. Its lethal purpose also suggests the blurry line for a sociopath between shooting with a camera and shooting to kill*

The film opens with a massacre—a drug deal gone bad near the Mexican border. A Vietnam vet named Moss, driving along in a pickup truck, comes upon the scene. While looking to see if anyone is still alive, he finds a bag containing millions of dollars, and takes off with it. Chigurh is hired by the cartel to stop Moss.

Like many Westerns before it, this is a chase story. But the West in which *No Country for Old Men* takes place is a wasteland of gas stations and cheap motels. And the gun Chigurh uses is not the six-shooter of old Westerns, bringing justice and peace to a wild land, but a gun from the slaughterhouse capable of shattering the skulls of cattle (see Figure 9.2). The camera shooting the film seems benign in comparison.

No Country for Old Men poses questions about the culture of rugged individualism by depicting its extreme. Chigurh pollutes the world with the horror of his indifference. He is not greedy like the man he is trailing, Moss, who is trying to steal the drug lords' money to make a new start in life. Chigurh is also not trying to be a drug lord. He is simply fulfilling a contract, and working in a community of strangers with the mechanistic and inhuman relentlessness of a machine.

This film raises the question of whether collective life is possible in a modern world dominated by neoliberal values, where contracts and self-maximization are not mitigated by the concept of a social contract or the common good. Chigurh is a game player, weighing probabilities like a computer in a military simulation. And he forces his victims to play with him. With the flip of a coin, they either live or die. Chigurh's way of computing his next move is indifferent, denying the mutual dependence underlying the social contract. In making a self and life according to neoliberal criteria, he denies the power of human will or the relevance of desire.

The film has a sheriff, Ed Tom Bell (Tommy Lee Jones), an aging witness to the struggle between Moss and Chigurh. He finds himself faced with a sociopath he cannot stop. He has no hope of enforcing the rule of law or restoring moral reasoning, so he is afraid. He is the old man whose country has been stolen. He is silenced by the relentlessness of a man who is a killing machine.

The only person who is not afraid to speak back to Chigurh is Moss' wife, Carla Jean (Kelly Macdonald). Chigurh tells her to toss a coin to have a chance to live. She refuses to do it, denying that life and death are merely chance opposites. She talks to him about his ability to make choices, calling on him to be a moral actor. But he leaves her place alone, presumably killing her.

No Country for Old Men serves as a thought experiment about the danger of extreme individualism, contractual relations, and the use of game-theoretical reasoning indifferent to moral considerations. It is a story that depicts the distance between neoliberal conceptions of modernity and the principles of modernity in Hollywood's American West. In *No Country for Old Men*, modern individualism has become so extreme that it has destroyed all possibility of a social contract and escape from tyranny.

EINSTEIN'S WIFE

Einstein's Wife is a documentary that explores the power of modern discourses of gender and science to erase from the historical record important contributions of women to science. It tells the story of Mileva Marić, Albert Einstein's first wife, a physicist who worked with him on his early papers (see Figure 9.3).[7] These were the ones from his "miracle year" in Zurich that made him famous and gained him a Nobel Prize. *Einstein's Wife* poses an extreme question: what if Mileva Marić co-authored the greatest papers in physics of the early 20th century? It makes the question credible by providing both evidence of their collaboration

FIGURE 9.3 *Mileva Marić and Albert Einstein, 1912*

---

[7] Svetlana Alter, *Secret Traces of the Soul of Mileva Maric-Einstein* (Pittsburgh, PA: Dorrance Publishing, 2003).

and descriptions of how Marić was erased from the history of science—lost behind the Einstein legend.

Einstein's Wife in part reveals the power of the complementarity thesis for gender. In the film, when physicists are asked about Marić and her role in Einstein's papers, they often describe her as Einstein's helpmate, not his collaborator. He is a genius; she is a helpful wife. She is not permitted to take even a small part of his legend, so Marić is lost behind the story of Einstein's heroic genius.[8]

Marić and Einstein met in graduate school in Zurich, the only two studying theoretical physics. She was the good student who went to classes, while he did not. She also worked in a laboratory in Germany gathering data relevant to their papers, while he stayed in Zurich, working in the Patent Office because he could not get a better job. She excelled in mathematics, but she did not pass her graduate exams. He did pass. So, his career in physics was the only one the couple could pursue.

Einstein's Wife focuses mainly on the extent to which they worked together on the papers from his "miracle year". They were married at the time, and they corresponded when they were apart about the problems in the papers. Abram Joffe, a Russian scientist, also said that he was asked to look at one of the great papers from 1905 before it was published, and testified that it originally included both the names Einstein and Marić. But Marić's name did not appear on the final publication. Was she also an author or even the primary author? Perhaps. We only know that Einstein gave her the money from the Nobel Prize, changing the money through a series of different currencies to hide the transfer.

Only after Einstein's death did his letters to Marić resurface. He had kept his relationship to her secret even to close friends in Princeton, who were surprised to know he had been married during his years in Zurich. The stories of him as a lone genius, struggling with great problems while working in the Patent Office, were easier to sustain this way. So, he hid all traces of her. And this indifference to her life and fate was all the more poignant on film because it was visibly intentional—in contrast to the indifference of the medium that told her story without malice.

WHERE THE HEART IS

Where the Heart Is is a drama about Wal-Mart and a homeless woman, raising questions about modern materialism. The heroine of the film, Novalee Nation, is abandoned at the store by her boyfriend (see Figure 9.4). With nowhere to go and pregnant, she hides among the commodities of modernity, depending on the periodic kindness of strangers to survive. The film is a "what if?" story about the role of commodities in modern life taken to an extreme. Novalee has nothing, and enters an emporium of things. As she makes a

---

[8] Pam Stello, "Why Defend Einstein's Reputation as a Lone Genius?" Unpublished paper, 2011.

FIGURE 9.4 *Novalee abandoned in the parking lot of Wal-Mart, contrasting the power of commerce and her powerlessness*

life in the store, the film becomes a thought experiment about the extent to which consumer goods can contribute to human welfare. It shows them compensating for failures of Novalee's relationships, but not being quite enough to sustain human life.

The film is a comforting tale about homelessness told in a medium whose own indifferent presence can comfort and distract. *Where the Heart Is* lulls us into smiling, with charming pictures of Novalee curling up to sleep next to a child's light in Wal-Mart. In this film, the relentlessness of the medium parallels the growth of her baby, and the indifference of the technology is as comforting as the commodities she "borrows" to survive in the store.

Novalee starts to live in Wal-Mart by mistake. The store closes while she is in the bathroom. So, she stays and sleeps there—warm, comfortable, and dry. The clothes, bedding, food, and magazines in Wal-Mart are more reliable than her boyfriend, and they fill the emptiness of her life. Novalee sleeps in a sleeping bag at night, uses an alarm clock to wake up and hide before the cleaning crew arrives, eats from the food counter, keeping track of what she owes, does baby exercises in the aisles, following instructions from a book (see Figure 9.5), and leaves the store to walk around the town during the day. Her problem is finding people in America to trust enough to leave Wal-Mart.

FIGURE 9.5 *Novalee doing prenatal exercises in Wal-Mart, demonstrating the power of modern things to provide comfort and aid to even the most destitute*

FIGURE 9.6 *Novalee and her baby, Americus Nation, waiting for Novalee's mother who never comes. She has stolen the money, and deserted them*

Novalee needs a community and meets people who are kind to her, including a woman named Thelma who gives her a tree, and the librarian, Forney, who looks after her. She does not fully trust them, but she has to give birth sometime, and cannot do this alone. Forney follows her to the store and when she goes into labor, passing out on the floor, he breaks into Wal-Mart and takes her to the hospital.

Novalee wakes up in a hospital bed as the mother of the "Wal-Mart" baby. She has an identity, money from the store to start her life, and a job offer from Wal-Mart. Novalee's mother, pretending to want to help, arrives in the hospital, but only takes the money, continuing the pattern of betrayal that plagues Novalee (see Figure 9.6).

As her life unfolds, the young innocent protagonist is witness to many more failed connections and cruelties. She builds a community of strangers, but her friends suffer betrayals, too. People are unreliable; things are not. So, Novalee finds pleasure in simple things like beds, magazines, trees, baby clothes, and dinner. She finds beauty in the indifference of modern things, mirroring the pleasure of film viewers who watch as light plays indifferently but innocently on the screen.

INDEPENDENCE DAY

Independence Day is an action/adventure film that raises questions about technological progress and military power by exploring an extreme story of war: the threat of human annihilation by aliens. It seems formulaic, but *Independence Day* exposes the foundations of modern life in utter destruction—devastation that requires ingenuity and self-fashioning. The film won an academy award for its special effects, using military technology to blow things up on screen. But the film was a morality tale about the illusory character of military power, using the visual impact of special effects to emphasize the limits of military might.

Action/adventure films, although often decried for their mindlessness, can do philosophical work by exploring the power and limits of technology. They are not stupid even when they are formulaic. They provide journeys into the uncanny—worlds of adventure and danger that are at once both recognizable and unfamiliar. The films embody fears about progress and ask "what if?" questions about technology, including whether weapons really do protect us from enemies and what the destructive power of technology does to people.

There is not much of a plot to *Independence Day*. It begins with an alien attack that targets cities around the world. The fate of the earth depends on the intelligence of a computer wizard, David Levinson (Jeff Goldblum), and the nerves of steel and sheer competence of two pilots, Captain Steven Hiller (Will Smith) and Russell Cass (Randy Quaid). The President Whitmore (Bill Pullman) is also a former pilot who tries to use weapons to save the day. The President orders a nuclear attack on the aliens, but that does nothing. The alien weapons they face are more powerful than those of all the world's armies. Hiller takes an enemy ship through the Grand Canyon (see Figure 9.7) to crash it, capturing the alien pilot, but the alien escapes. Levinson suggests implanting a virus in their computer system, and by this method reduces the power of their shields. This allows the navy pilots to start a nuclear blast in the mother ship that destroys it.

Independence Day seems on one level just a celebration of masculinity, foregrounding the strong bodies and tough character of working-class men, and the nerdy intelligence of men of science. But the film is more importantly a "what if?" story about modernity and war. Once the White House is blown up (see Figure 9.8), the characters are stripped of the illusion of progress and have no weapons adequate to prove their power, so they have to get creative

FIGURE 9.7 *Still of the Grand Canyon. Hiller takes the alien through the Grand Canyon*

FIGURE 9.8 *The White House being blown up, suggesting the failure of states to maintain power simply with weapons*

about restoring life, liberty, and happiness. In the terms of the philosophical experiments with the Defecating Duck, they must depend on their "souls" rather than on machines.

Independence Day was a showcase of American military prowess even though the military finally refused to provide personnel and technical support for the project because the director insisted on a segment about Area 51, an "alien research site." The special effects were nonetheless mainly displays of military explosives that asserted the power of shock and awe in battle. At the same time, the film told a tale about the futility of depending on weapons, and the illusion of power an arsenal could create. The result was an uncanny story about the rebirth of the modern values through military violence, and a tale about the illusory quality of military power told through a medium reproducing those illusions.

Independence Day was massively popular not only because the special effects were good and Will Smith was an attractive hero, but also because it seemed to reaffirm American values and opened in time for 4th of July celebrations. It celebrated American character as necessary for defending freedom. In this sense, it was a simple piece of ideology. But the film was not so simple, as it used special effects to display as well as describe the illusory nature of military power.

THOUGHT EXPERIMENTS AND PHILOSOPHICAL MACHINES

Thought experiments on film are forms of cultural imagination that allow people to think critically about their culture by putting it in extra-human form. By following out the implications of "what if?" questions in narratives, they can probe the culture and let viewers assess it. Like Riskin's Defecating Duck, films pose problems rather than argue a case, and in doing so, they provide points of cultural reflexivity.

Such fictions are not propaganda because they are not designed to promote a point of view, but rather use the indifference of film, the comfort it can provide and the illusions it can convey to pose questions about human beings, social connectivity, and cultural imaginaries. Filmic thought experiments are popular because they probe a moral landscape in deeply engaging and disturbing ways. They show rather than tell. And they raise questions about what it means to be human by holding the human stories on the screen against the relentless indifference of mechanical or digitized movement of light.

CHAPTER TEN

ESCAPE ROUTES AND RESTLESSNESS

Modernity is painful and modern life is demanding. The categories cut, the personal restlessness never ends, the accounting and accountability are oppressive, the drive for profits is corrosive, extracting property from nature is destroying the planet, despotism seems just as resilient as democracy, secularists battle with spiritual believers, technologies alienate as well as give pleasure, racial hatred abounds, women are subject to violence, robots replace workers, people use mobile technology to blow themselves up in crowds of strangers, and time moves on anyhow. So, modern people want to get out, opt out—escape.

But escape from what? What could escape from modernity possibly mean? Modernity seems only a reification: an abstract concept treated as real. It has no site or clear marker. There is nothing tangible, no iron cage of modernity to flee from, so what is there to escape? The simple answer: injurious discursive traditions and dangerous material practices. The colonization of consciousness by discourse, the destruction of millions of people in modern wars, and the degradation of the earth for industrial "progress" are plenty to escape.

If a culture is a complex of activities, objects, institutional structures, and standards of practice, it is held together by logics and logics of practice, vague ways of dreaming, or vigorous ways of reasoning about what is, could be, or might be made. These logics are incessantly reworked as they are imagined, debated, and embodied in things, so culture is dynamic and encompassing. This makes modernity more like a whirlwind than a cage; it sucks up the earth wherever it goes and is hard to escape or see beyond.

The modern desire to escape was encapsulated and satirized in one of the first novels: Jonathan Swift's *Gulliver's Travels*.[1] Going to sea was a metaphor for escaping modernity, a way of noting and ridiculing the posturing and emptiness of modern life. Swift's hero, Gulliver, took to the sea to explore foreign kingdoms, but as he traveled from one ineffective polity to another, he witnessed the same kinds of foolishness of rulers and political

---

[1] Jonathan Swift, *Gulliver's Travels* (Ireland: Joseph Pearce, 1726).

FIGURE 10.1 *Richard Redgrave,* Gulliver in Brobdingnag, *1836*

regimes as in Europe (see Figure 10.1). Escape was necessary to imagine for Swift, but the escape routes for Gulliver were false exits.

People feel caught in modernity in ways they cannot articulate. The practices of everyday self- and world-making come with limited instructions. There are choreographies to enact, ways to claim selfhood, expectations to fill, standards to meet, mistakes to make, and dangers to avoid, but the cultural logics they embody are obscure.[2] As Mead[3] suggests, modern people learn who they are by practicing their parts. They engage in ordinary activities until they know them well enough that they no longer have to think about them. They use kinesthetic knowledge to act appropriately without self-consciousness.[4] These performances are scaffolded by the material order and discourse

---

[2] Erving Goffman, *Presentation of Self in Everyday Life* (Garden City, NY: Doubleday Anchor, 1959).

[3] George Herbert Mead, *On Social Psychology: Selected Papers,* rev. edn (Chicago: University of Chicago Press, 1964).

[4] David Sudnow, *Ways of the Hand* (Cambridge, MA: Harvard University Press, 1978); Jean Lave, *Understanding Practice: Perspectives on Activity and Context* (Cambridge and New York: Cambridge University Press, 1993); Morana Alac, *Handling Digital Brains: A Laboratory Study of Multimodal Semiotic Interaction in the Age of Computers* (Cambridge, MA: MIT Press, 2011).

that defines what is "appropriate." As people cook meals, walk paths or streets, drive a car, or play an instrument, the cultural logics of modernity guide them, but the rules of conduct fall from consciousness.[5] This leaves people feeling caught in routines, wanting to flee without knowing why.

Nietzsche[6] thought modernity created a form of collective amnesia. People internalized values, and found themselves unaware of *why* they held the values they did: "We knowers are unknown to ourselves … honey gatherers of the mind."[7] Simply responding to things in a culturally programmed way was dangerous, Nietzsche thought. People would willingly embrace values that served others at their own expense. Following the "rule of freedom," they would reproduce a culture designed to oppress them.[8]

Growing up within a cultural community or habitus, Bourdieu added,[9] members of groups develop cultural predispositions that they act upon without reasoning. They acquire the tastes expected of them, but experience their preferences as quite personal and genuine—both heartfelt and common sense. So, they follow their tastes, but in doing so, demonstrate social subordination more than agency.[10]

The modern self is a way of performing an identity as an agent, using material means to assert importance and taking personal responsibility for actions. It is not a social role, but a logic of being in the world that people both enact and seek.[11] Modernity is a "figured world"[12] of culture that is dreamt up and imagined, enacted and materialized, but a figured

[5] Erving Goffman, *Behavior in Public Places* (New York: Free Press, 1963).

[6] Friedrich Nietzsche, *The Birth of Tragedy: And, the Genealogy of Morals*, trans. Francis Golffing (New York: Anchor Books, 1990).

[7] Nietzsche, *The Birth of Tragedy*, p. 149.

[8] Patrick Joyce, *The Rule of Freedom: Liberalism and the Modern City* (London and New York: Verso, 2003); Jeffrey Minson, *Genealogies of Morals* (London: Palgrave Macmillan, 1988).

[9] Pierre Bourdieu, *Distinction: A Social Critique of the Judgment of Taste*, trans. Richard Nice (London: Routledge and Kegan Paul, 1984); Bourdieu (with Luc Boltanski), *Photography, a Middle-Brow Art*, trans. Shaun Whiteside (Stanford: Stanford University Press, 1990).

[10] Raymond Williams, *Sociology of Culture* (Chicago: University of Chicago Press, 1981); Richard Hebdige, *Subculture: The Meaning of Style* (London: Methuen, 1979); Stuart Hall, *Representation* (London: Sage, 1997).

[11] George Herbert Mead, *On Social Psychology: Selected Papers*, rev. edn (Chicago: University of Chicago Press, 1964); Peter Berger and Thomas Luckmann, *The Social Construction of Reality* (Garden City, NY: Anchor Books, 1967); Gary Allen Fine, *Tiny Publics* (New York: Russell Sage, 2012); Barrie Thorne, "'Childhood': Changing and Dissonant Meanings," *International Journal of Learning and Media* (2009), 1(1): 1–9; Nina Eliasoph, *Avoiding Politics* (Cambridge: Cambridge University Press, 1998); Paul Lichterman, *The Search for Political Community* (Cambridge: Cambridge University Press, 1996); Sherry Ortner, *Anthropology and Social Theory: Culture, Power, and the Acting Subject* (Durham and London: Duke University Press, 2006); Donna Jeanne Haraway, *Primate Visions: Gender, Race, and Nature in the World of Modern Science* (New York: Routledge, 1989); Paul Lichterman, *The Search for Political Community* (Cambridge: Cambridge University Press, 1996).

[12] Dorothy Holland, William S. Lachicotte, Jr., Debra Skinner, and Carole Cain, *Identity and Agency in Cultural Worlds* (Cambridge, MA: Harvard University, 1998).

world in motion—unstable, mobile, transforming, and world making.[13] The logics of modernity at the level of selves, communities, and states are entangled,[14] bound together in braids continually twisting around cultural imaginaries and discursive principles.[15]

The consequences are very different if cultural logics are played out in pursuit of cultural imaginaries or according to discursive principles. Cultural imaginaries can unfold in a variety of ways, so they allow experiments with life paths and support improvised patterns of everyday life. Principles, in contrast, determine legitimacy. Consider an example. The citizen as a cultural imaginary is part of an imagined community whose actions determine what a citizen might do or claim to be. The citizen as a legal (discursive) category provides criteria for determining belonging or exclusion.

The range of actions possible in the pursuit of cultural imaginaries is large. If Americans, for example, imagine that they live in the "land of the free and home of the brave," they can test their bravery and fight for their freedom, whatever those terms might mean to them. They might join the army, go to Wall Street, fight for social justice, take mind-altering drugs, run a theater troupe, travel around the world, or start a business, but they will engage in these very different activities using similar logics of self-affirmation and identity formation. They will follow well-worn paths for enacting freedom and displaying bravery, adorning themselves in appropriate costumes for their social journeys, adopting the language for describing themselves as "free and brave," and creating places to live and work freely and bravely. The cultural logic remains the same, but as an imaginary it can be elaborated in a range of ways.

The difference between cultural imaginaries and principles helps explain why the articulation of modern principles in the 17th and 18th centuries changed modernity, and made it less of an experiment and more of a political weapon. Being modern had always entailed living in history, making a life, and claiming a social identity. But principles of progress created hierarchies of social types, defined some ways of life as better than others, and entangled states in geopolitical struggles for dominance.[16]

It was not supposed to be this way. Enlightenment debates about modernity were meant to build better societies and polities. Defining best practices in education or government was expected to improve human conduct and quality of life. But as ideals were turned into measures of success, criteria of adequacy became tools of exclusion. Internalized as practices, discursive modernity colonized consciousness. People started to follow

---

[13] See Holland et al., *Identity and Agency*. See also Lilly Irani, J. Vertesi, Paul Dourish, Kevita Philip, and Rebecca E. Grinter, "Post-Colonial Computing," *Proceeding of the SIGCHI* (Atlanta, GA: ACM, 2010), pp. 1311–20.

[14] Karen Michelle Barad, *Meeting the Universe Halfway: Quantum Physics and the Entanglement of Matter and Meaning* (Durham: Duke University Press, 2007).

[15] Geoffrey C. Bowker and Susan Leigh Star, *Sorting Things Out: Classification and Its Consequences* (Cambridge, MA: MIT Press, 1999).

[16] Minson, *Genealogies of Morals.*

the logics of ideas they never debated, and to inhabit a discursive culture they did not fully understand. By displacing rather than serving human rationality and equality, discursive modernity created reasons to escape it.

Deleuze[17] has explained why this is not so easy. The problem of modern life is that we are blinded by the categories that both inspire and constrain us. If we reason with our categories and internalize them, we lose the ability to feel and dream outside the parameters imposed by language. We are too entangled cognitively with the language of discursive common sense to challenge it. We have to flee into inarticulacy and the illogical to imagine other worlds and invent other words.

Much of modern art and politics has been devoted to this project: pursuing forms of inarticulacy to make meaning problematic and stir the imagination. Experiments with silence in music, locating architecture underground, using drugs to feel things that cannot be said, or parading through streets for social justice all do not "make sense" if you want to "get things done," but neither are they random. They are experiments in escaping the limitations of modern discourse.

AESTHETIC ESCAPE ROUTES

Many experiments in inarticulate modernity have been aesthetic, ways of feeling a path beyond common sense. William Blake's books and Humphry Davy's drug experiments were early examples. They tried to experience the sublime— a force of life, nature, and imagination they could not fully comprehend with words. These Romantics and others rejected the idea that reason was the defining characteristic of human beings, finding humanity in the unspeakable beauty and horror of deep feeling.

William Morris struggled to escape common sense another way. He wanted to evade forms of economic reasoning that he saw as soul crushing. He countered liberal ideas of property and progress by mass-producing goods for people without money. The point was political. He was a socialist, and wanted to usc goods to give dignity to the working class. Beautiful consumer goods were markers of social worth that the poor could not afford, so Morris provided them with books, wallpaper (see Figure 10.2), curtains, tiles, and furniture that were inexpensive and stunning. He explored what socialism might mean as a practice rather than as an idea. The beautiful figures on his textiles and books did not tell

FIGURE 10.2 *William Morris, Wallpaper design, 1862*

---

[17] Gilles Deleuze, *Difference and Repetition* (New York: Columbia University Press, 1994).

people what to think, but rather engaged them in politics by "other means".[18] Designing industrial goods for socialist purposes made no sense, but that is why it gained attention to his cause.[19]

Modern artists in the 20th century have also plumbed the depths of inarticulacy to find freedom beyond discursive common sense. For example, the composer John Cage used silence to escape the categories of music and of the concert. As he sat impassively in front of a piano, he drew attention to listening as an activity and ambient sounds as interesting. Cage created disturbing, funny, and moving experiences by making the rational tonalities and rhythms of concert music disappear, collapsing music-making and listening beyond common sense.[20]

Similarly, when Jackson Pollock threw paint on canvas rolled out onto the ground, he evaded common-sense understandings of artistic practice. He did not make himself visible as an artist, leaving evidence of his painterly hand in the texture of the paint. Pollock threw paint at the canvas, and used the flight of the paint—its life between artist and canvas—to make layered ribbons of color that had depth and complexity. He stepped onto the canvas, too, refusing to distinguish the artist from what he made. Pollock claimed the result of his practice was not accidental, but it was not planned. Painting for Pollock was a process, what he called direct painting. Streams of paint were thrown about, and developed their own accommodations to each other. Pollock made art by becoming entangled with the paint and canvas in new ways. The result was inarticulate and gestural, demonstrating what else it was possible to do with paint.[21]

Maya Lin also played with inarticulacy in the Vietnam War Memorial (see Figure 10.3). She wanted to create an environment to serve grieving, supporting the human feeling of loss, so she took her architecture underground to the level of graves. The Memorial was less a work of architecture than a passageway through memory that moved visitors as they moved through it.

The Memorial listed the names of all of those who died in the Vietnam War on a long wall of dark stone along a ramp descending into the earth. Beneath the grass and trees, visitors could look for the names of friends or relatives they had lost. The inarticulacy of the Memorial matched the silence of the dead. And the facade of unmoving names stood in contrast to the living that walked by or wept. The Memorial demonstrated rather than represented the separation that death created, and that war had brought to so many.[22]

---

[18] Haraway, *Primate Visions*.

[19] Fiona MacCarthy, *Anarchy and Beauty: William Morris and His Legacy, 1860–1960* (New Haven: Yale University Press, 2014).

[20] John Cage, *Silences* (Middletown, CT: Wesleyan University Press, 1939); Alexandra Munroe, *The Third Mind: American Artists Contemplate Asia, 1860–1989* (New York: Guggenheim Foundation, 2009), pp. 199–215.

[21] Ellen Landau, *Jackson Pollock* (New York: Harry Abrams, 2010); Frank O'Hara, *Jackson Pollock* (Sevenoaks, UK: Pickle Partners Publishing, 2015).

[22] Maya Ying Lin, *Boundaries* (New York: Simon & Schuster, 2000).

FIGURE 10.3 *Maya Lin, Vietnam War Memorial*

Modern artists who turned away from discursive modernity did not stop it, but demonstrated the escape routes. They showed the value of defying common sense, violating standards, experimenting with their hands and ears, and finding something beyond words in their humanity. They took liberties to find freedom, and showed that this modern principle had other possibilities beyond common sense. Their experiments, tricks, jokes, and silent excursions into imagination stood in contrast to the petty tyrannies and inequalities of modern life, and their celebrations of common humanity stood in contrast to the contemporary privatization of the commons.[23]

POLITICAL ESCAPE ROUTES

Perhaps ironically, those who most want to be free of modernity also have been the people that most value its principles: freedom, opportunity, human rights, free labor, religious tolerance, and the pursuit of the common good. Many have found neoliberal calculation exclusionary and heartless as an approach to life in contrast to these values.[24] Others have mourned the fact that nationalism leads so quickly and often to military

---

[23] Tarleton Gillespie, *Wired Shut* (Cambridge, MA: MIT Press, 2007).
[24] Margaret Somers, *Genealogies of Citizenship* (Cambridge: Cambridge University Press, 2008).

violence.[25] In response to these and other injuries, groups have formed social justice movements to question the ways modern principles have been translated into practices. They have staged demonstrations that might seem "meaningless," but they create social networks of activists and constituencies supporting their dreams.[26] In pointing to injuries of modernity that are not easily articulated and creating forms of connectivity that defy common sense, they conjure up escape routes from the present—mostly utopian but sometimes dystopian, too.[27]

Seeking escape routes through social action, protesting the false promises of modernity, has been a tradition in America. Henry David Thoreau's *Walden; or Life in the Woods*[28] described one man's effort to flee from modern materiality and standards of good conduct. Thoreau turned his back on the good people of Concord to live among trees, birds, bugs, and seasons. He did not want to make progress, accumulate property, and live politely among strangers. He wanted direct access to the world, and immersed himself in the silence of the woods. He built a small shelter by Walden Pond (see Figure 10.4), and ridiculed his neighbors for their fine houses and possessions. Thoreau recognized the desperation in their materialism and mutual surveillance. They were invested in modern ideas of property and improvement. But he preferred the silence of the woods, learning from nature rather than exploiting it. He moved beyond reason and discursive common sense to learn through sensibility and contemplation.

The counterculture in the US in the 1960s was deeply influenced by Thoreau, and imitated his move back to the country as a form of cultural critique. The generation that came of age in the 1960s was raised during the Cold War, witness to the frightening specter of hostile nations with nuclear weapons. It was educated by the Civil Rights movement, too, witness to the legacy of race-based slavery (see Figure 10.5).

Modernity in that moment looked particularly dangerous to human bodies. So, young people started a range of social justice movements that spread around the world. In 1968 in France, the students aligned with workers, threatening to overturn normal political processes. In the Eastern Bloc, students advocated liberal freedoms in spite of the futility of demanding them there. In most of these movements, people did the unthinkable, and were met with violent government suppression. But still they made a difference.[29] They

[25] Mabel Berezin, *Making the Fascist Self: The Political Culture of Interwar Italy* (Ithaca, NY: Cornell University Press, 1997); Simonetta Falasca-Zamponi, *Fascist Spectacle: The Aesthetics of Power in Mussolini's Italy* (Berkeley: University of California Press, 1997).

[26] Claude Rosental, "Toward a Sociology of Public Demonstrations," *Sociological Theory* (2013), 31(4): 343–65.

[27] Bennett Berger, *Survival of a Counterculture* (Berkeley and Los Angeles: University of California Press, 1981); John R. Hall, *Apocalypse Observed* (London: Routledge, 2000).

[28] Henry David Thoreau, *Walden; or, Life in the Woods* (Boston, MA: Ticknor and Fields, 1854).

[29] Anna Szemere, *Up from the Underground: The Culture of Rock Music in Post-Socialist Hungary* (University Park, PA: Pennsylvania State University Press, 2001).

FIGURE 10.4 *Walden Pond*

FIGURE 10.5 *Dr. Martin Luther and Coretta Scott King in a Civil Rights March*

FIGURE 10.6 *Drag Queen Float in Gay Pride Parade, San Francisco*

acted in defiance of common sense, asking what sense the political order made in its current form.[30]

Both Black Power groups and the Women's Movement emerged from these early protests, but the majority of their followers turned to Civil Rights legislation and voters' rights as means of redress. So, the Gay Pride movement became the social justice movement that most effectively used inarticulate politics. Gay Pride activists wanted to bring out of the closet LGBT communities that had never counted or been counted, and make the damage caused by homophobia visible in the streets.

The playful spectacle at the Gay Pride Parade in San Francisco (see Figure 10.6), showing that queer could be queerer than straight people could imagine, embodied and parodied performances of gender and sexuality. Instead of hiding, LGBT people strutted and capered their way down streets, taking over public spaces even where it was dangerous. The political spectacle was inarticulate, but the calls for social justice were heard, and began to make sense to most Americans.[31]

The Occupy Movement followed in the same tradition, starting with political theater expressing discontent with the economic status quo. The movement began with Occupy

---

[30] Todd Gitlin, *The Sixties: Years of Hope, Days of Rage* (New York: Bantam, 1989).

[31] John Loughery, *The Other Side of Silence* (New York: Henry Holt and Company, 1998), chapter 7.

Wall Street in 2011 in the wake of the stock market crash of 2008. Occupy Wall Street activists questioned the massive economic and social inequality that Wall Street helped to produce, but never paid for. Wall Street had been bailed out, but Main Street had to flounder. In the absence of any way of debating economic issues with experts, Occupy Wall Street protesters simply occupied Zuccotti Park, setting up a tent city in the land of high finance. They camped out, listened to speakers, and tried to find better ways to live together. They drew attention to inequality with a simple phrase: the 99 percent vs. the 1 percent. The 99 percent was the bulk of people in America without wealth, and the 1 percent was the corporate elite taking an increasing share of the pie. The injustice was clear, but how to hold people accountable for inequality was not; Occupy protesters put the problem on the public agenda not by arguing the case, but by refusing to go home.[32] And it worked—not directly but dramatically. Their insistence on redress for inequality found its way into the political agenda of Bernie Sanders in seeking the presidency.

Black Lives Matter has been particularly effective in using video rather than discourse to draw attention to unspeakable patterns of violence against Black youth. Not able to argue that they were being mistreated by police, African–Americans started making pictures and videos of police aggression, posting them online. The videos showed a policeman shooting Tamir Rice, a 12-year-old boy sitting on a swing, and depicted Michael Brown apparently shot while running away from the police. There was nothing to say about these acts; no need for discourse so far from common sense—only justice. Like Gay Pride activists, Black Lives Matter protesters made patterns of violence visible, and police forces started to put cameras on helmets and cars to document encounters.[33]

The Arab Spring was comparably a way of pointing to the massive inequalities of modern states, but seemed to have the opposite political effects, leading to repression and disorder rather than progressive change. People took to the street to protest the betrayals of modern principles by corrupt political leaders in Arab countries. It began in one of the more modern North African countries, Tunisia, when a street vendor, Tarek el-Tayeb Mohammed Bouazizi, refused to pay a bribe and had his goods confiscated for it. He set fire to himself in an act of resistance that gave others courage. Protests broke out, first in Tunisia, and then in much of the Arab world. In Egypt, demonstrators with similar grievances camped out in Tahir Square, seeming to win a victory when Mubarak was ousted and Egypt had elections (see Figure 10.7).

The problem was that there was a large chasm between the inarticulate, liberal dreams of those camped on the street and the political discourse of the Muslim Brotherhood elected to office and charged with writing up a constitution. Not happy with the anti-modernist discourse of the government, the military staged a coup, bringing in a new wave of repression. Words failed, force prevailed, collapse ensued, but memories lingered.[34]

---

[32] http://occupywallst.org/

[33] Kelly Gates, "The Work of Wearing Cameras: Police Media Work and the Police Media Economy," in Richard Maxwell (ed.), *Routledge Companion to Labor and Media* (New York: Routledge, 2015), pp. 252–64.

[34] Jeffrey C. Alexander, *Performative Revolution in Egypt* (New York: Bloomsbury Academic, 2011).

FIGURE 10.7 *Tahir Square, February 8, 2011*

These political movements, using inarticulate means of calling for social justice, have had varying results—legal and political. They have all violated discursive common sense to create change, appearing naive and foolish. But participants dreamt of realizing principles of modernity, and showed how these principles were being compromised by practices. They insisted on freedom from tyranny and human rights, and began to imagine what that might mean. They held out hope for better versions of modern life, better interpretations of modern principle, and more agency for modern individuals. So even when they failed, they pointed to escape routes from the painful perversions of modernity, pointing to futures that could be different.

ESCAPING MATERIAL MODERNITY

Forms of material or embodied modernity can be as destructive as discourse, but they are harder to remedy. Modern progress is obviously embodied in skyscrapers and weapons, factories, nightclubs, subway systems, airports, national monuments, fast road systems, and fast-food joints. Less clearly, modernity's failures are as material as its successes, manifested in urban slums and ghettos, areas like Chernobyl ruined by a nuclear accident, and farmland depleted by scientific farming methods.[35] Modern selves continue to construct identities with clothes, build communities with infrastructure, differentiate states with national art and armories, and use industry and trading infrastructures to shape global capitalism. In many ways, modernity has become self-perpetuating because the architecture and infrastructure that surround people embody and promote modern versions of common sense. Languages of progress have been embedded in bridges, bullet trains, wind farms, and urban development. But they are not articulate, so they engage in politics beyond words.

This makes it hard for people to counter or modify the material destruction of modern progress: the plantation agriculture, polluted cities, strip mines, and factories that destroy land, undermine old ways of life, and force more people to reinvent themselves. Sea levels are now rising because of modern material practices, threatening to displace large numbers of coastal residents, and wars testing the relative modernity of states are scattering refugees around the world. The destructive aspects of material modernity are visibly changing social worlds, and some people want a way out of the injuries and dangers.

Critiques of materiality tend to be almost laughably limited in addressing these issues because most do not attend to the devastation of landscape and bodies. Centered in neo-Marxist works, they are mostly critiques of consumption and commodity fetishism—a very small part of the grand transformation of modern material worlds.[36] We might expect Marx to address the silent, physical forms of destructiveness in capitalism, but he locates the political problem of modernity in capitalist social relations, arguing against attention to things in themselves. The terrible environmental devastation in East Bloc countries under communism is easy to explain because of Marx's championing of unfettered technological development. Modernity under communism may have developed without modern property relations, but in the pursuit of industrial modernity, it was just as destructive to people and things.[37]

Material forms themselves are silent, so while they act politically, they do so beyond debate. It is not clear what they "mean," so it is not clear what the remedy should be. A material order like a ghetto, a concentration camp, a city with no housing for the poor, patterns of industrial agriculture, over-grazed forests, or weak states plagued by vigilante

---

[35] Loïc Wacquant, *Urban Outcasts* (Cambridge: Polity Press, 2008); Olga Kuchinskaya, *The Politics of Invisibility* (Cambridge, MA: MIT Press, 2014); David R. Montgomery, *Dirt: The Erosion of Civilizations* (Berkeley and Los Angeles: University of California Press, 2007), chapter 10; Marisa Brandt, "Zapatista Corn: A Case Study in Biocultural Innovation," *Social Studies of Science* (2014), 44(6): 874–900.

[36] Daniel Miller, *Material Culture and Consumerism* (New York: Basil Blackwell, 1987); George Ritzer, *McDonaldization of Society* (Newberry Park, CA: Pine Forge Press, 1993). For an exception, see Geneviève Zubrzycki, *The Crosses of Auschwitz* (Chicago: University of Chicago Press, 2006).

[37] Virág Molnár, *Building the State* (Abingdon, UK and New York: Routledge, 2013).

violence create social injustice, but make redress more difficult because the injuries are silent and their sources hard to trace.[38]

My husband likes to tell a story about a developer who was refused a permit for a building project because there was an eagle's nest in a tree on the property. So, he came with a bulldozer at night and knocked down the tree, destroying the nest. Perhaps the builder paid a fine, but he certainly got his permit. And there was no remedy; even taking him to court would not restore the tree and nest. And when he applied for the permit a second time, there was nothing left on his land to protect.[39]

As I have argued before, there are two kinds of power—strategic and logistic.[40] Political wrangling at the level of ideology and law is strategic, and proceeds through debate: forms of articulation or discourse. Logistical power is the power derived from material activity, changing the physical environment in which social life takes place. And as much as some want to escape the tyranny of discourse, others want a way out of destructive patterns of logistical progress. They pursue the latter by finding language for describing what material rationality has wrought, using discourse to counter the silences.

As early as the mid-19th century, George P. Marsh[41] was writing about the material destruction of "civilization" from Rome into modernity. He called his book an environmental geography, looking at effects of material practices on places. He argued that humans certainly had a right, like all animals, to create a livable habitat by affecting the space around them. Humans had a right to cut forests to make fields, for example, but not to engage in heedless destruction of the earth. He was particularly opposed to the arrogant disregard of the destructive qualities of modern industry and war. A century later, Rachel Carson[42] echoed his sentiments when she wrote on the environmental damage caused by commercial agriculture and the use of pesticides. The combination of war and lax regulation of industry had become endemic to modernity, and threatened the health of citizens. Modern life was meant to promote human well-being, but was failing at that mission.

Writers have used their words to give voice to the dead and to land destroyed by human greed and negligence. Kai Erikson, for example, in *Everything In Its Path*, described a set of dams that had not been properly maintained that broke in a narrow valley where miners and their families lived. The resulting flood tore away the town and most of those who lived there.

---

[38] Charles Tilly, *Politics of Collective Violence* (Cambridge: Cambridge University Press, 2003).

[39] Thanks to Zachary Fisk for this story.

[40] Chandra Mukerji, "The Territorial State as a Figured World of Power: Strategics, Logistics and Impersonal Rule," *Sociological Theory* (2010), 28(4): 402–25.

[41] George P. Marsh, *Man and Nature: or Physical Geography as Modified by Human Action* (Seattle and London: University of Washington Press, [1864] 2004).

[42] Rachel Carson, *Silent Spring* (New York: Houghton Mifflin, 1962).

The disaster stretched human nerves to their outer edge. Those of us who did not experience it can never really comprehend the full horror of that day, but we can at least appreciate why it should cause such misery and why it should leave so deep a scar on the minds of those who lived through it. Our imagination can reach across the gulf of personal experience and begin to re-create those parts of the scene that touch the senses. Our eyes can almost see a burning black wave lashing down the hollow and taking everything in its path. The ears can almost hear a roar like thunder, pierced by screams and explosions and the crack of breaking timbers. The nostrils can almost smell the searing stench of mine wastes and the sour odor of smoke and death and decay. All this we can begin to picture because the mind is good at imagery.[43]

Words such as these cannot undo the damage, but they can still hold the events in memory, and point to those accountable for the tragedy. It does not save the families, town, or trees in the hollow, but it provides relief from the indifferent silence and provides language for political redress.

The Eichmann trial was another effort to create some form of discursive accountability—this time, for the horror of industrial slaughter of human life in concentration camps (see Figure 10.8). The legal proceedings turned memories into testimony, rumor into legal fact. Hannah Arendt retold the story, as did Val Hartouni.[44] Each told a different tale with an alternate moral to the story. But witnesses at Eichmann's trial as well as commentators raised questions of accountability by putting silent acts of cruelty into words (see Figure 10.9).

Arendt named the evil as banal, bureaucratic, and consummately modern. Eichmann was a pawn in an anti-Semitic regime. Hartouni insisted that genocide was a modern political practice, less a product of German anti-Semitism than of political calculation. Either reading put the horror in words. The testimony at the trial and the ensuing debate could not determine the truth or change what happened, but it provided support for the efforts of the International Court at The Hague to hold leaders accountable for genocide by translating unspoken and unspeakable cruelties into legal discourse.

Another kind of voicing of injuries came from South Africa with the Truth and Reconciliation tribunals.[45] The apartheid system was a modern means of sanctioning systematic oppression, exploitation, rancor, and sectarian cruelty by allocating assets, spaces, and rights disproportionately by race. Its power lay in its brutality and banality—the impersonal measures, and violently maintained borders between groups.[46] The system was

---

[43] Kai Erikson, *Everything In Its Path: Destruction of Community in the Buffalo Creek Flood* (New York: Simon and Schuster, 1976).

[44] Hannah Arendt, *Eichmann in Jerusalem* (New York: Viking Press, 1963); Valerie Hartouni, *Visualizing Atrocity* (New York: New York University Press, 2012).

[45] Robert Britt Horwitz, *Communication and Democratic Reform in South Africa. Communication, Society, and Politics* (Cambridge and New York: Cambridge University Press, 2001).

[46] Bowker and Star, *Sorting Things Out.*

FIGURE 10.8 *A Family Arriving at Auschwitz-Birkenau Concentration Camp*

horrific and traumatizing even to those who perpetrated it—although obviously worse for their victims. So, after apartheid was abolished, the country found itself relieved of the system of oppression, but not the memories and silences that still haunted people. South Africa needed a way to heal. Truth and reconciliation tribunals were the answer the government chose, turning acts of destruction into words of penance. In these tribunals, perpetrators of atrocities were required to give voice to what they had done. The point was to pierce the silence, force confessions, make killers recognize the damage they had done, allowing the country as a whole to grieve for South Africa's damaged soul and lost lives.

Most of the injuries of material modernity are not so dramatic. There are neglected neighborhoods where buildings that were once modern have deteriorated. There are factory towns without work. And there are neighborhoods with polluted water supplies, and toxic soil from closed factories or uranium mines.[47] The injuries also include the incessant micro-aggressions that deplete selves, hurt communities, and threaten lives: the routine harassment of women and minorities on the street, and the daily slights and wounds of LGBT people denied bathrooms. These are the small wounds that remind groups that they are vulnerable. Most injuries of this sort are never voiced. Neglect and harassment

---

[47] Gabriel Hecht, *Being Nuclear: Africans and the Global Uranium Trade* (Cambridge, MA: MIT Press, 2012).

often silence people. But not completely. Bloggers and poet activists speak out, reclaiming their dignity and asserting their humanity by telling their stories.[48]

Other forms of articulation are used to focus on losses in nature rather than human life resulting from practices of material modernity. The growth of environmental economics, for example, is tied to the need to debate environmental protection as a political issue and to litigate cases of pollution like oil spills.[49] Measures and regulation relating to climate change are also ways of trying to make the human effect on the planet a policy matter that has to be addressed. But as has been clear in American politics, describing climate change with words and numbers does not stabilize its meaning. On the contrary, it stimulates arguments. Still, the Paris Agreement of 2015 on climate change, whether it will have environmental benefits or not in the long run, at least gives language to the problem and provides measures of accountability. It does not contain a clear escape route from catastrophic environmental change, but suggests how to proceed in that direction.

FIGURE 10.9 *Eichmann in Ramle Prison, 1961*

THE RESTLESS SELF AND GRIEF

The desire to escape is as old as modernity itself. Even before discursive standards were put in place to distinguish those who were truly modern from those who were not, and before the monuments of material modernity multiplied the injuries to people and things, the burden of personal responsibility for one's destiny made life difficult, and life among strangers made people restless. Modern life became global partly out of this restlessness as people moved, impelled by dreams of escape, or they became refugees from the violence of making modern worlds.

Modernity began as a response to grief and remains a mode of destroying worlds while seeking new directions. Modernity requires repair work, and the need for repair is often hidden to maintain the illusion of forward movement.[50] Modern things are

---

[48] Jennifer Vernon, *Rock Candy* (New York: West End Press, 2009); Stephanie Berger, *In the Madame's Hatbox* (New York: Dancing Girl Press, 2011); www.tumblr.com/tagged/microaggression

[49] Marion Fourcade, "Cents and Sensibility: Economic Values and the Nature of 'Nature' in France and America," *American Journal of Sociology* (2011), 116(6): 1721–77.

[50] Christopher Henke, "The Mechanics of Workplace Order: Toward a Sociology of Repair," *Berkeley Journal of Sociology* (2000), 44(4): 55–81.

not stable. Bridges rust, factories and prisons are abandoned, neighborhoods rot, walls collapse, streets become full of potholes, and wires fall on country roads. The crumbling areas are hidden behind the new neighborhoods, streets, highways, and cities. As McDonnell and Dominguez Rubio[51] have shown, material modernity is always in process, things transforming as well as people. Bruno Latour[52] has called the modern period a great experiment with the planet that is now revealing its limits. Things are transforming in ways we cannot stop.

Modern individuals at the birth of modernity in the plague initiated the pattern of restlessness and grief. They sought ways of recovering from the losses and injury to their old lives. They searched around for ways of healing, changing the material order to do so. The restless drive into the future, the sense of grief and search for material comfort became the source of the braiding, unbraiding, and rebraiding of modernity that continues today. Seeking escape routes is a way to acknowledge this grief and point to the injuries inflicted by modern patterns of geopolitics. And seeking escape routes is a way to organize the restlessness of self-fashioning subjects who want to remake themselves and modernity itself. Seeking escape routes is a way to change the principles of modernity so that freedom has new meanings and purposes. And seeking escape routes is a way of following principles of practice to decide what can be done next.

The braiding and rebraiding of modernity pulls in new stands, and ties back others that fall out. The point is to give people something to grab onto as they improvise selves and lives. This braid is Ariadne's thread—something to hold while moving forward, a logic of taking responsibility for history, and fleeing from destructive words and deeds. It is not for going backwards, seeking escape as Theseus did. In the modern world, history only goes in one direction. Escape is the restlessness of a morning, opening the door and stepping out.

---

[51] Fernando Dominguez Rubio and Elizabeth Silva, "Materials in the Field: Object Trajectories and Object-Positions in the Field of Contemporary Art," *Cultural Sociology* (2013), 7: 161–78; Fernando Dominguez Rubio, "Preserving the Unpreservable: Docile and Unruly Objects at MoMA," *Theory and Society* (2014), 43(6): 617–45; Terence McDonnell, *Best Laid Plans* (Chicago: University of Chicago Press, 2016).

[52] Bruno Latour, *Reset Modernity: Fieldbook* (Karlsruhe: Center for Art and Media Karlsruhe, 2016).

APPENDIX

TEACHING RESOURCES

This book is derived in part from lectures that I have given in classes, so I see it as well suited for classroom use. To help instructors, I have assembled a set of historical materials and developed pedagogical exercises based on them that instructors can use (or not). These are located on the publisher's website associated with this book: www.routledge. com/cw/mukerji.

This archive mainly contains images about fashion, art, race, gender, and industrial factories and cities. But it also has links to other archives of humanist writings and YouTube videos that readers can use to examine the kinds of cultural objects described in the book. The archive is a resource for studying modernity that I think anyone might enjoy; the exercises I have written are there to develop a better understanding of the arguments. I hope instructors who do not like the exercises will think up their own ways of using the archives. Evidence of the past lies in pictures and texts, waiting for new eyes to glance their way. The imaginaries that are key to the history of modernity are embedded in pictures and sounds that can barely be touched upon in a short book.

Bibliography

Adams, Julia, *The Familial State* (Ithaca: Cornell University Press, 2005).

Alac, Morana, *Handling Digital Brains: A Laboratory Study of Multimodal Semiotic Interaction in the Age of Computers* (Cambridge, MA: MIT Press, 2011).

Alexander, Jeffrey, *Performative Revolution in Egypt* (New York: Bloomsbury Academic, 2011).

Alter, Svetlana, *Secret Traces of the Soul of Mileva Maric-Einstein* (Pittsburgh, PA: Dorrance Publishing, 2003).

Anderson, Benedict, *Imagined Communities: Reflections on the Origins and Spread of Nationalism* (London: Verso, 1983).

Arendt, Hannah, *Eichmann in Jerusalem* (New York: Viking Press, 1963).

Ariès, Philippe, *Centuries of Childhood: A Social History of Family Life*, trans. Robert Baldick (New York: Knopf, 1962).

Austen, Jane, *Pride and Prejudice* (New York: Penguin Classics, 2002).

Austen, Jane, *Sense and Sensibility* (New York: Penguin Classics, 2003).

Austen, Jane, *Mansfield Park* (New York: Penguin Classics, 2003).

Azurara, Gomes Eannes de, *The Chronicle of the Discovery and Conquest of Guinea, Vol. I*, trans. Charles Raymond Beazley and Edgar Prestage (New York: Burt Franklin Publisher, 1963).

Bakhtin, Mikhail, *Rabelais and His World* (Bloomington: Indiana University Press, 1984).

Ballon, Hillary, *The Paris of Henry IV: Architecture and Urbanism* (Cambridge: MIT Press, 1994).

Barad, Karen Michelle, *Meeting the Universe Halfway: Quantum Physics and the Entanglement of Matter and Meaning* (Durham: Duke University Press, 2007).

Barth, Gunther, *City People: The Rise of Modern City Culture in Nineteenth-Century America* (Oxford: Oxford University Press, 1980).

Bauman, Zygmunt, *Modernity and Ambivalence* (London: Polity Press, 1993).

Becker, Howard, *Art Worlds* (Berkeley: University of California Press, 1982).

Beik, William, *Absolutism and Society in Seventeenth Century France: State Power and Provincial Aristocracy in Languedoc* (Cambridge: Cambridge University Press, 1985).

Benzecry, Claude, *The Opera Fanatic* (Chicago: University of Chicago Press, 2011).

Berezin, Mabel, *Making the Fascist Self: The Political Culture of Interwar Italy* (Ithaca, NY: Cornell University Press, 1997).

Berger, Bennett, *Survival of a Counterculture* (Berkeley and Los Angeles: University of California Press, 1981).

Berger, John, "The Suit and the Photograph," in Chandra Mukerji and Michael Schudson (eds), *Rethinking Popular Culture* (Berkeley and Los Angeles: University of California Press, 1991).

Berger, Peter and Thomas Luckmann, *The Social Construction of Reality* (Garden City, NY: Anchor Books, 1967).

Berger, Stephanie, *In the Madame's Hatbox* (New York: Dancing Girl Press, 2011).

Bernasconi, Robert and Tommy L. Lott, *The Idea of Race* (Indianapolis: Hackett Publishing, 2000).

Biernacki, Richard, *The Fabrication of Labor* (Berkeley and Los Angeles: University of California Press, 1997).

Billington, James, *The Icon and the Axe: An Interpretative History of Russian Culture* (New York: Random House, 2010), Kindle edition.

Blaeu, Joan, *Atlas Maior of 1665*, ed. Peter Van Der Krogt (Köin: Taschen, 2005).

Blake, William, *Songs of Innocence and Experience*. Copy B, 1789, 1794 (British Museum) electronic edition. www.blakearchive.org/exist/blake/archive/copy.xq?copyid=sonsie.b&java=no

Bloch, Marc, *French Rural History: An Essay on its Basic Characteristics*, trans. Janet Sondheimer (London: Routledge and Kegan Paul, 1978).

Boccaccio, Giovanni, *The Decameron*, trans. Mark Musa and Peter Bondanella (New York: Norton, 1977).

Bourdieu, Pierre (with Luc Boltanski) *Photography, a Middle-Brow Art*, trans. Shaun Whiteside (Stanford: Stanford University Press, 1990).

Bourdieu, Pierre, *Distinction: A Social Critique of the Judgment of Taste*, trans. Richard Nice (London: Routledge and Kegan Paul, 1984).

Bowker, Geoffrey C. and Susan Leigh Star, *Sorting Things Out: Classification and Its Consequences* (Cambridge, MA: MIT Press, 1999).

Boyer, John, *The University of Chicago: A History* (Chicago: University of Chicago Press, 2015).

Brandt, Marisa, "Zapatista Corn: A Case Study in Biocultural Innovation," *Social Studies of Science* (2014), 44(6): 874–900.

Brandt, Marisa, *War, Trauma and Technologies of the Self: Making of Virtual Reality Exposure Therapy*. Dissertation, University of California, San Diego, 2013.

Brown, Jonathan, *Painting in Spain, 1500–1700* (New Haven: Yale University Press, 1998).

Burke, Peter, *Popular Culture in Early Modern Europe* (London: Temple Smith, 1978).

Burke, Peter, *The Fabrication of Louis XIV* (Bath: The Bath Press, 1994).

Butler, Judith, *Bodies that Matter* (New York: Routledge, 1993).

Cage, John, *Silences* (Middletown, CT: Wesleyan University Press, 1939).

Carson, Rachel, *Silent Spring* (New York: Houghton Mifflin, 1962).

Cook, Harold, *Matters of Exchange: Commerce, Medicine, and Science in the Dutch Golden Age* (New Haven: Yale University Press, 2007).

Cosgrove, Denis, "Mapping New Worlds: Culture and Cartography in Sixteenth-Century Venice," *Imago Mundi* (1992), 44(1): 65–89.

Craveri, Benedetta, *The Age of Conversation*, trans. Teresa Waugh (New York: New York Review of Books, 2005).

Crenshaw, Kimberly, "Demarginalizing the Intersection of Race and Sex," *University of Chicago Racial Forum* (1989), 140(1): 139–67.

Cressy, David, "Literacy in Pre-Industrial England," *Societas* (1974), 4: 229–40.

Cronon, William, *Nature's Metropolis: Chicago and the Great West* (New York: W.W. Norton & Company, 1992).

Darnton, Robert, *The Great Cat Massacre, and Other Episodes in French Cultural History* (New York: Basic Books, 1999).

Daufresne, Jean-Claude, *Louvre & Tuileries: Architectures de Papier* (Bruxelles: Pierre Mardaga, 1987).

Davis, Natalie Zemon, *Society and Culture in Early Modern France* (Stanford: Stanford University Press, 1975).

Davis, Natalie Zemon, *The Return of Martin Guerre* (Cambridge, MA: Harvard University Press, 1983).

BIBLIOGRAPHY

Deleuze, Gilles, *Cinema 1: The Movement Image* (London: Athlone Press, 1986).

Deleuze, Gilles, *Cinema 2: The Time Image* (Minneapolis: University of Minnesota Press, 1989).

Deleuze, Gilles, *Difference and Repetition* (New York: Columbia University Press, 1994).

Dewey, John, *Experience and Education* (New York: Free Press, 1997).

Dobbin, Frank, *Forging Industrial Policy: The United States, Britain, and France in the Railway Age* (Cambridge: Cambridge University Press, 1994).

Dominguez Rubio, Fernando and Elizabeth Silva, "Materials in the Field: Object Trajectories and Object-Positions in the Field of Contemporary Art," *Cultural Sociology* (2013), 7(2): 161–78.

Dominguez Rubio, Fernando, "Preserving the Unpreservable: Docile and Unruly Objects at MoMA," *Theory and Society* (2014), 43(6): 617–45.

Douglas, Mary, "Jokes," in Chandra Mukerji and Michael Schudson (eds), *Rethinking Popular Culture* (Berkeley and Los Angeles: University of California Press, 1991), pp. 291–310.

Dutta, Krishna, *Calcutta: A Cultural History* (Oxford: Signal Books, 2003).

Edwards, Paul, *The Closed World and the Politics of Discourse in Cold War America* (Cambridge, MA: MIT Press, 1996).

Eisenstein, Elizabeth, *The Printing Press as an Agent of Change: Communication and Cultural Transformation in Early Modern Europe*, vols I and II (Cambridge: Cambridge University Press, 1979).

Elias, Norbert, *The Court Society*, trans. Edmund Jephcott (Dublin: University of Dublin Press, 1969).

Elias, Norbert, *The Civilizing Process*, vol. I (New York: Pantheon Books, 1982).

Eliasoph, Nina, *Avoiding Politics* (Cambridge: Cambridge University Press, 1998).

Elliot, J. H., *The Old World and the New* (Cambridge University Press, 1970).

Enenkel, Karl, Betsy de Jong-Crane and Peter Liebgrets, *Modelling the Individual* (Amsterdam: Rodopi, 1998).

Erikson, Eric, *Childhood and Society* (New York: Norton, 1950).

Erikson, Kai, *Everything in Its Path: Destruction of Community in the Buffalo Creek Flood* (New York: Simon and Schuster, 1976).

Escher, M. C., *M. C. Escher: The Graphic Work* (New York: Taschen America, 1992).

Falasca-Zamponi, Simonetta, *Fascist Spectacle: The Aesthetics of Power in Mussolini's Italy* (Berkeley: University of California Press, 1997).

Fine, Gary Allen, *Tiny Publics* (New York: Russell Sage, 2012).

Foucault, Michel, *The Order of Things; An Archeology of the Human Sciences* (New York: Penguin Books, 1971).

Fourcade, Marion, "Cents and Sensibility: Economic Values and the Nature of 'Nature' in France and America," *American Journal of Sociology* (2011), 116(6): 1721–77.

Fournier, Edward, *Histoire du Pont-Neuf* (Paris: E. Dentu, 1862).

Fuller, Margaret, *Woman in the Nineteenth Century* (New York: Greeley & McElrath, 1845), p. 174.
https://archive.org/details/womaninnineteent1845full

Gardner, Howard, *The Quest for Mind: Piaget, Levi-Strauss and the Structuralist Movement* (Chicago: University of Chicago, 1981).

Gates, Kelly, "The Work of Wearing Cameras: Police Media Work and the Police Media Economy," in Richard Maxwell (ed.), *Routledge Companion to Labor and Media* (New York: Routledge, 2015), pp. 252–64.

Gazzard, Alison, *Mazes in Videogames: Meaning, Metaphor and Design* (Jefferson, NC and London: McFarland & Company, Inc., 2013).

Geisel, Theodore (Dr. Seuss), *Cat in the Hat* (New York: Random House, 1957).

Gilchrist, Alexander, *Life of William Blake* (London: John Lane, 1907), Kindle edition.

Gillespie, Tarleton, *Wired Shut* (Cambridge, MA: MIT Press, 2007).

Ginzburg, Carlo, *The Cheese and the Worms: The Cosmos of a Sixteenth-Century Miller* (Baltimore: Johns Hopkins University Press, 1992).

Gitlin, Todd, *The Sixties: Years of Hope, Days of Rage* (New York: Bantam, 1989).

Goffman, Erving, *Presentation of Self in Everyday Life* (Garden City, NY: Doubleday Anchor, 1959).

Goffman, Erving, *Behavior in Public Places* (New York: Free Press, 1963).

Goldstein, Claire, *Vaux and Versailles* (Philadelphia: University of Pennsylvania Press, 2008).

Golinski, Jan, *The Experimental Self: Humphry Davy and the Making of a Man of Science* (Chicago: University of Chicago Press, 2016).

Goody, Jack, *The Logic of Writing and the Organization of Society* (Cambridge: Cambridge University Press, 1986).

Granovetter, Mark, "The Strength of Weak Ties," *American Journal of Sociology* (May 1973), 78(6): 1360–80.

Gray, Herman, *Watching Race* (Minneapolis: University of Minnesota Press, 2004).

Greenfield, Sidney M., "Madeira and the Beginnings of New World Sugar Cane Cultivation and Plantation Slavery: A Study in Institution Building," *Annals of the New York Academy of Sciences* (1977), 292: 536–52.

Hall, John R., *Apocalypse Observed* (London: Routledge, 2000).

Hall, Stuart, *Representation* (London: Sage, 1997).

Haraway, Donna Jeanne, *Primate Visions: Gender, Race, and Nature in the World of Modern Science* (New York: Routledge, 1989).

Harrison, Carol E. and Ann Johnson, *National Identity: The Role of Science and Technology* (*Osiris* series, 24(1)) (Chicago: University of Chicago Press, 2009).

Hartouni, Valerie, *Visualizing Atrocity* (New York: New York University Press, 2012).

Harvey, David, *Spaces of Capital: Towards a Critical Geography* (New York: Routledge, 2001).

Harvey, David, *Paris: Capital of Modernity* (New York and London: Routledge, 2003).

Hebdige, Dick, *Subculture: The Meaning of Style* (London: Methuen, 1979).

Hecht, Gabrielle, *Being Nuclear: Africans and the Global Uranium Trade* (Cambridge, MA: MIT Press, 2012).

Henke, Christopher, "The Mechanics of Workplace Order: Toward a Sociology of Repair," *Berkeley Journal of Sociology* (2000), 44(4): 55–81.

Hennion, Antoine and J.-M. Fouquet, *Grandeur de Bach: L'Amour de la Musique en France au XIXe Siècle* (Paris: Fayard, 2000).

Herlihy, David, *The Black Death and the Transformation of the West*, ed. Samuel K. Cohn, Jr. (Cambridge, MA: Harvard University Press, 1997).

Hirschman, Nancy and Kirstie McClure, *Feminist Interpretations of John Locke* (University Park, PA: Pennsylvania State University Press, 2007).

Hobbes, Thomas, *Leviathan*, ed. C. MacPherson (London: Penguin Classics, 1982).

Holland, Dorothy, William S. Lachicotte, Jr., Debra Skinner, and Carole Cain, *Identity and Agency in Cultural Worlds* (Cambridge, MA: Harvard University, 1998).

Horwitz, Robert Britt, *Communication and Democratic Reform in South Africa.* (Cambridge and New York: Cambridge University Press, 2001).

Huizinga, Johan, *Homo Ludens: The Study of the Play Element in Culture* (London: Routledge & Kegan Paul, 1955).

Huppert, George, *After the Black Death: A Social History of Early Modern Europe*, 2nd edition (Bloomington: Indiana University Press, 1998).

Ikegami, Eiko, "Visualizing the Networked Self: Agency, Reflexivity and the Social Life of Avatars," *Social Research* (2011), 78(4): 1155–84.

Irani, Lilly, J. Vertesi, Paul Dourish, Kevita Philip, and Rebecca E. Grinter, "Post-Colonial Computing," *Proceeding of the SIGCHI* (Atlanta, GA: ACM, 2010), pp. 1311–20.

Isaac, Benjamin, *The Invention of Racism in Classical Antiquity* (Princeton: Princeton University Press, 2004).

Johnson, Sara E., *The Fear of French Negroes* (Berkeley and Los Angeles: University of California Press, 2012).

Jones, Ann Rosalind and Peter Stallybrass, *Renaissance Clothing and the Materials of Memory* (Cambridge: Cambridge University Press, 2000).

Jonnes, Jill, *Eiffel's Tower: The Thrilling Story Behind Paris's Beloved Monument and the Extraordinary World's Fair That Introduced It* (New York: Penguin Books, 2009).

Jordan, David, *Transforming Paris: The Life and Labors of Baron Haussmann* (New York: Free Press, 1995).

Jordan, Jennifer A., *Structures of Memory: Understanding Urban Change in Berlin and Beyond* (Stanford: Stanford University Press, 2006).

Joyce, Patrick, *The Rule of Freedom: Liberalism and the Modern City* (London and New York: Verso, 2003).

Joyce, Patrick, *The State of Freedom* (Cambridge: Cambridge University Press, 2013).

Kelly, John, *The Great Morality: An Intimate History of the Black Death, the Most Devastating Plague of All Time* (New York: HarperCollins, 2005).

Knorr-Cetina, Karin, *Epistemic Cultures* (Cambridge, MA: Harvard University Press, 1999).

Krasner, Stephen, *Sovereignty* (Princeton, NJ: Princeton University Press, 1999).

Kuchinskaya, Olga, *The Politics of Invisibility* (Cambridge, MA: MIT Press, 2014).

La Gorce, Jérôme de, *Dans l'Atelier des Menus Plaisirs du Roi. Spectacles, Fêtes et Cérémonies aux XVIIe et XVIIIe Siècles* (Paris: Archives Nationales-Versailles, Artlys, 2010).

Lamont, Michèle (ed.) *Cultural Territories of Race: Black and White Boundaries* (Chicago: University of Chicago Press, 1999).

Lamont, Michèle, *The Dignity of Working Men* (Cambridge, MA: Russell Sage Foundation, 2000).

Landau, Ellen, *Jackson Pollock* (New York: Harry Abrams, 2010).

Langins, Janis, *Conserving the Enlightenment* (Cambridge, MA: MIT Press, 2004).

Lareau, Annette, *Unequal Childhoods: Class, Race, and Family Life* (Berkeley and Los Angeles: University of California Press, 2011).

Latour, Bruno, *We Have Never Been Modern* (Cambridge, MA: Harvard University Press, 1993).

Latour, Bruno, *Reset Modernity: Fieldbook* (Karlsruhe: Center for Art and Media Karlsruhe, 2016).

Lave, Jean, *Understanding Practice: Perspectives on Activity and Context* (Cambridge and New York: Cambridge University Press, 1993).

Lefebvre, Henri, *The Production of Space* (Oxford and Cambridge, MA: Blackwell, 1991).

Lenoir, Tim and Henry Lowood, "Theaters of War: The Military-Entertainment Complex," http://web.stanford.edu/class/sts145/Library/Lenoir-Lowood_TheatersOfWar.pdf

Levesque, Antoine, *Receuil de Decorations de Theatre par Monsieur Levesque, Garde General des Magasins des Menus Plaisirs de la Chambre* (Paris: Archives Nationales, 1752), CP/O/1/3238.

Lichterman, Paul, *The Search for Political Community* (Cambridge: Cambridge University Press, 1996).

Lin, Maya Ying, *Boundaries* (New York: Simon & Schuster, 2000).

Lipsitz, George, *Time Passages: Collective Memory and American Popular Culture* (University of Minnesota Press, 1990).

Lipsitz, George, *How Racism Takes Place* (Minneapolis; Philadelphia: Temple University Press, 1990; 2011).

Lipton, Sarah, *Dark Mirror: The Medieval Origins of Anti-Jewish Iconography* (New York: Macmillan, 2014), Kindle edition.

Locke, John, *The John Locke Collection: 6 Classic Works* (Charleston, SC: Waxkeep Publishing, 2013).

Lockridge, Kenneth, *Literacy in Colonial New England* (New York: Norton, 1974).

Lough, John, *France Observed in the Seventeenth Century by British Travelers* (Boston: Oriel Press, 1985).

Loughery, John, *The Other Side of Silence* (New York: Henry Holt and Company, 1998).

Loyrette, Henri, Sebastian Allard, and Laurence Des Cars (eds), *Nineteenth Century French Art: From Romanticism to Impressionism, Post-Impressionism, and Art Nouveau*, trans. David Radzinowicz (Paris: Flammarion, 2007).

Luker, Kristin, *When Sex Goes to School* (New York: W.W. Norton, 2006).

MacCarthy, Fiona, *Anarchy and Beauty: William Morris and His Legacy, 1860–1960* (New Haven: Yale University Press, 2014).

McCarthy, Cormac, *No Country for Old Men* (New York: Vintage International, 2005).

McCullough, David Willis, *The Unending Mystery* (New York: Random House, 2004).

McDonnell, Terence, *Best Laid Plans* (Chicago: University of Chicago Press, 2016).

Machiavelli, Niccolò, *The Prince*, trans. Donno (New York: Bantam, 1966).

McKendrick, Neil, John Brewer, and J. H. Plumb, *The Birth of a Consumer Society: Commercialization of Eighteenth-Century England* (Bloomington: Indiana University Press, 1982).

McNeill, William H., *Plagues and Peoples* (New York: Anchor Books, 1976).

Magubane, Zine, "American Sociology's Racial Ontology: Remembering Slavery, Deconstructing Modernity, and Charting the Future of Global Historical Sociology," *Cultural Sociology*, online, May 6, 2016.

Manguel, Alberto, *A History of Reading* (London: Penguin, 1996).

Manning, Alex, Douglas Hartmann, and Joseph Gerteis, "Colorblindness in Black and White: An Analysis of Core Tenets, Configurations and Complexities," *Sociology of Race and Ethnicity* (2015), 1(4): 532–46.

Mantoux, Paul, *The Industrial Revolution in the Eighteenth Century* (London: Jonathan Cape, revised edition, 1961).

Marsh, George P., *Man and Nature: Or Physical Geography as Modified by Human Action* (Seattle and London: University of Washington Press, [1864] 2004).

Martin, Karin A., "Becoming a Gendered Body: Practices of Pre-Schools," *American Sociological Review* (1998), 63(4): 494–511.

Marx, Karl and Friedrich Engels, *Capital* (New York: International Publishers, 1967).

Mead, George Herbert, *On Social Psychology: Selected Papers*, revised edition (Chicago: University of Chicago Press, 1964).

Meyers, Peter Alexander, *Abandoned to Ourselves* (New Haven: Yale, 2013).

Michael, D. and S. Chen, *Serious Games* (Boston, MA: Thompson Course Technology, 2006).

Miller, Daniel, *Material Culture and Consumerism* (New York: Basil Blackwell, 1987).

Minson, Jeffrey, *Genealogies of Morals* (London and New York: Palgrave Macmillan, 1988).

Mitford, Nancy and Liesl Schillinger, *Frederick the Great* (New York: Penguin, Random House, 2013), Kindle edition.

Molnár, Virág, *Building the State* (Abingdon, UK and New York: Routledge, 2013).

Montessori, Maria, *The Secret of Childhood* (New York: Ballantine Books, 1982).

Montgomery, David R., *Dirt: The Erosion of Civilizations* (Berkeley and Los Angeles: University of California Press, 2007).

Mukerji, Chandra, *From Graven Images: Patterns of Modern Materialism* (New York: Columbia University Press, 1983).

Mukerji, Chandra, *Territorial Ambitions and the Gardens of Versailles* (Cambridge: Cambridge University Press, 1997).

Mukerji, Chandra, "Material Practices of Domination: Christian Humanism, the Built Environment, and Techniques of Western Power," *Theory and Society* (Feb. 2002), 31(1): 1–34.

Mukerji, Chandra, "The Territorial State as a Figured World of Power: Strategics, Logistics and Impersonal Rule," *Sociological Theory* (2010), 28(4): 402–25.

Mukerji, Chandra, "Jurisdiction, Inscriptions and State Formation," *Theory and Society* (2011), 40(3): 223–45.

Mukerji, Chandra, "Space and Political Pedagogy at the Gardens of Versailles," *Public Culture* (2012), 24(3), 68: 509–34.

Mukerji, Chandra and Tarleton Gillespie, "Recognizable Ambiguity: Cartoon Imagery and American Childhood in Animaniacs," in Dan Cook (ed.), *Symbolic Childhood* (New York: Peter Lang Publishers, 2002), pp. 227–54.

Mukherjee, Prithwindra, *Les Racines Intellectuelles du Mouvement d'Indépendance de l'Inde (1893–1918)* (Talmont St. Hillaire: Éditions Codex, 2014).

Munroe, Alexandra, *The Third Mind: American Artists Contemplate Asia, 1860–1989* (New York: Guggenheim Foundation, 2009).

Nash, Jennifer, "Rethinking Intersectionality," *Feminist Review* (2008), 89: 1–15.

Neff, Gina, *Venture Labor: Work and the Burden of Risk in Innovative Industries* (Cambridge, MA: MIT Press, 2012).

Nelson, William Max, "Making Men: Enlightenment Ideas of Racial Engineering," *American Historical Review* (Dec. 2010), 115(5): 1364–91.

BIBLIOGRAPHY

Neraudau, Jean-Pierre, *L'Olympe du Roi-Soleil: Mythologie et Ideologie Royale au Grand Siècle* (Paris: Les Belles Lettres, 1986).

Newman, Karen, *Cultural Capitals: Early Modern London and Paris* (Princeton: Princeton University Press, 2007).

Nicolay, Nicolas de, *Dans l'Empire de Soliman le Magnifique* (Paris: Presses du CNRS, 1989).

Nietzsche, Friedrich, *The Birth of Tragedy and the Genealogy of Morals*, trans. Francis Golffing (New York: Anchor Books, 1990).

O'Hara, Frank, *Jackson Pollock* (Sevenoaks, UK: Pickle Partners Publishing, 2015).

Oreskes, Naomi, "Objectivity or Heroism?" *Osiris* (1996), 11: 87–113.

Ortner, Sherry, *Anthropology and Social Theory: Culture, Power, and the Acting Subject* (Durham and London: Duke University Press, 2006).

Palma, Michael, Hans Adler, Johann Herder, and Ernest Menze, *Johann Gottfried Herder on World History: An Anthology* (New York and London: Routledge), Digital edition.

Pandora, Katherine, "The Children's Republic of Science in the Antebellum Literature of Samuel Griswold Goodrich and Jacob Abbott," ed. Carol E. Harrison and Ann Johnson, *Osiris* (2009), 24.

Patterson, Orlando, *Slavery and Social Death: A Comparative Study* (Cambridge, MA: Harvard University Press, 1982).

Patterson, Orlando, *Rituals of Blood* (Washington, DC: Civitas/Counterpoint, 1998).

Peck, Reece, "You Say Rich, I Say Job Creator," *Media Culture and Society* (May 2014), 36(4): 526–35.

Peiss, Kathy, *Cheap Amusements: Working Women and Leisure in Turn-of-the-Century New York* (Philadelphia: Temple University Press, 1986).

Perrault, Charles, Sébastien Le Clerc, and Michel Conan, *Le Labyrinthe de Versailles 1677* (Paris: Editions du Moniteur, 1982).

Petrach, Francesco, *Familial Letters*, and *The Complete Conzoniere*, trans. and annotated A. S. Kline (Manchester: Poetry in Translation, 2001).

Piaget, Jean, *The Early Growth of Logic in the Child* (London: Routledge and Kegan Paul, 1959).

Postman, Neil, *The Disappearance of Childhood* (New York: Delacorte Press, 1982).

Prakash, Gyan, *Another Reason: Science and the Imagination of Modern India* (Princeton: Princeton University Press, 1999).

Prensky, Marc, "True Believers: Digital Game-Based Learning in the Military," in Prensky, *Digital Game-Based Learning* (New York: McGraw-Hill, 2001).

Quillian, Lincoln and Devah Pager, "Black Neighbors, Higher Crime? The Role of Racial Stereotypes in Evaluations of Neighborhood Crime," *American Journal of Sociology* (2001), 107(3): 717–67.

Raj, Kapil, *Relocating Modern Science: Circulation and the Construction of Knowledge in South Asia and Europe, 1650–1900* (New York: Palgrave Macmillan, 2007).

Raj, Kapil, "Régler les Différends, Gérer les Différences: Dynamiques Urbaines et Savantes à Calcutta au XVIIe Siècle," *Revue d'Histoire Moderne et Contemporaine* (2008), 55(2): 70–100.

Ramond, Pierre, *André-Charles Boulle, Ébéniste, Cisleleur & Carqueteur Ordinaire du Roy* (Dourdan: Vial, 2011).

Rafael, Vincente, *White Love and Other Events in Filipino History* (Durham and London: Duke University Press, 2000).

Riskin, Jessica, "The Defecating Duck, or the Ambiguous Origins of Artificial Life," *Critical Inquiry* (2003), 29(4): 599–633.

Riskin, Jessica, *Genesis Redux: Essays in the History and Philosophy of Artificial Life* (Chicago: University of Chicago Press, 2007).

Ritzer, George, *McDonaldization of Society* (Newberry Park, CA: Pine Forge Press, 1993).

Rojek, Chris, *The Labour of Leisure: The Culture of Free Time* (London: Sage, 2010).

Rörig, Fritz, *The Medieval Town* (Berkeley and Los Angeles: University of California Press, 1967).

Rosenau, Helen, *The Ideal City: Its Architectural Evolution in Europe* (New York: Methuen, 1982).

Rosental, Claude, "Toward a Sociology of Public Demonstrations," *Sociological Theory* (2013), 31(4): 343–65.

Rothrock, George, A., "The Musée des Plans-Reliefs," *French Historical Studies* (1969), 6(2): 253–6.

Rousseau, Jean-Jacques, *Émile* (New York: Heritage Illustrated Publishing, 2014), Kindle edition.

Sadkar, Myra and David Sadkar, *Failing at Fairness* (New York: Touchstone Books, 1994).

Said, Edward, *Orientalism* (New York: Pantheon, 1978).

Sammond, Nicholas, *Babes in Tomorrowland: Walt Disney and the Making of the American Child, 1930–1960* (Durham: Duke University Press, 2005).

Sanford, J. B., "Argument against Women's Suffrage, 1911." Prepared by J. B. Sanford, Chairman of the Democratic Caucus. Argument against senate constitutional amendment no. 8. http://stpl.org/pdf/libraries/main/sfhistory/suffrageagainst.pdf

Schama, Simon, *The Embarrassment of Riches: An Interpretation of Dutch Culture in the Golden Age* (New York: Knopf, 1987).

Shanley, Mary Lyndon, "Marriage Contract and Social Contract in Seventeenth-Century English Thought," in Nancy Hirschman and Kirstie McClure (eds), *Feminist Interpretations of John Locke* (University Park, PA: Pennsylvania State University Press, 2007), chapter 1.

Schiebinger, Londa, *The Mind Has No Sex? Women in the Origins of Modern Science* (Cambridge: Harvard University Press, 1991).

Schiebinger, Londa, *Nature's Body: Gender in the Making of Modern Science* (Boston, MA: Beacon Press, 1993).

Schochet, Gordon, "Models of Politics and the Place of Women in Locke's Political Thought," in Nancy Hirschman and Kirstie McClure (eds), *Feminist Interpretations of John Locke* (College Station: Pennsylvania State University Press, 2007), chapter 4.

Schutz, Alfred, *The Phenomenology of the Social World* (Evanston, IL: Northwestern University Press, 1970).

Sendak, Maurice, *Where the Wild Things Are* (New York: Harper and Row, 1963).

Serres, Olivier de, *Du Théatre d'Agriculture et Mesnage des Champs* (Paris: I. Méyater, 1600).

Sewell, William, "The Empire of Fashion and the Rise of Capitalism in 18th-Century France," *Past and Present* (2010), 206: 81–120.

Shaya, Gregory, "The Flâneur, the Badaud, and the Making of a Mass Public in France, circa 1860–1910," *The American Historical Review*, 109(1): 41–77.

Simmel, Georg, "The Metropolis and Mental Life," in Gary Bridge and Sophie Willson (eds), *The Blackwell City Reader* (Oxford and Walden, MA: Wiley-Blackwell, [1903] 2002).

Simmel, Georg, *The Sociology of Georg Simmel* (Glencoe, IL: Free Press, 1950).

Sims, Christo, "From Differentiated Use to Differentiating Practices," *Information, Communication and Society* 17(6): 670–82.

Sims, Christo, *The Cutting Edge of Fun* (Princeton: Princeton University Press, forthcoming).

Smith, Roger D., *Military Simulations and Serious Games* (Oviedo, FL: Modelbenders, 2009).

Soll, Jacob, *The Information Master: Jean-Baptiste Colbert's Secret State Intelligence System* (Ann Arbor: University of Michigan Press, 2009).

Somers, Margaret, *Genealogies of Citizenship* (Cambridge: Cambridge University Press, 2008).

Sparavigna, Amelia Carolina, "Ad Orientem: The Orientation of Gothic Cathedrals of France," http://arxiv.org/pdf/1209.2338.pdf

Star, Susan Leigh, "The Ethnography of Infrastructure," *American Behavioral Scientist* (1999), 43: 377–91.

Staum, Martin, *Labeling People: French Scholars on Society, Race, and Empire, 1815–1848* (Montreal and Kingston: McGill-Queen's University Press, 2003).

Steele, Claude, *Whistling Vivaldi* (New York: W.W. Norton, 2010).

Steiner, Rudolph, *Intuitive Thinking as a Spiritual Path: A Philosophy of Freedom*, trans. Michael Lipson (Hudson, NY: Anthroposophic Press, 1995).

Steinmetz, George, *State/Culture: State-Formation after the Cultural Turn* (Ithaca, NY: Cornell University Press, 1999).

BIBLIOGRAPHY

Steinmetz, George, *The Devil's Handwriting* (Chicago: University of Chicago Press, 2007).

Stello, Pam, "Why Defend Einstein's Reputation as a Lone Genius?" Unpublished paper, 2011.

Stern, Lesley, *The Smoking Book* (Chicago: University of Chicago Press, 1999).

Stern, Lesley, *Dead and Alive* (Montreal: Caboose, 2012).

Sudnow, David, *Ways of the Hand* (Cambridge, MA: Harvard University Press, 1978).

Sutton-Smith, Brian, *The Ambiguity of Play* (Cambridge, MA: Harvard University Press, 1997).

Surak, Kristin, *Making Tea, Making Japan* (Stanford: Stanford University Press, 2012).

Swift, Jonathan, *Gulliver's Travels* (Ireland: Joseph Pearce, 1726).

Szemere, Anna, *Up from the Underground: The Culture of Rock Music in Post-Socialist Hungary* (University Park, PA: Pennsylvania State University Press, 2001).

Thoreau, Henry David, *Walden; or, Life in the Woods* (Boston: Ticknor and Fields, 1854).

Thorne, Barrie, "'Childhood': Changing and Dissonant Meanings," *International Journal of Learning and Media* (2009), 1(1): 1–9.

Tilly, Charles, *Politics of Collective Violence* (Cambridge: Cambridge University Press, 2003).

Tsing, Anna. *The Mushroom at the End of the World* (Princeton: Princeton University Press, 2015).

Valls, Andrew, *Race and Racism in Modern Philosophy* (Ithaca: Cornell University Press, 2005).

Van Zanten, David, *Designing Paris: The Architecture of Duban, Labrouste, Duc, and Vaudoyer* (Cambridge, MA: MIT Press, 1987).

Veblen, Thorstein, *The Theory of the Leisure Class: An Economic Study of Institutions* (New York: Viking Press, 1945).

Vernon, Jennifer, *Rock Candy* (New York: West End Press, 2009).

Vygostky, L. S., *Mind in Society: The Development of Higher Psychological Processes*, ed. Michael Cole (Cambridge, MA: Harvard University Press, 1980).

Wacquant, Loïc, *Urban Outcasts* (Cambridge: Polity Press, 2008).

Wagner-Pacifici, *The Art of Surrender* (Chicago: University of Chicago Press, 2005).

Wagner-Pacifici, "Theorizing the Restlessness of Events," *American Journal of Sociology* (2010), 115(5): 1351–86.

Wallerstein, Immanuel, *The Modern World-System* (New York: Academic Press, 1974).

Walzer, Michael, *Revolution of the Saints* (Cambridge, MA: Harvard University Press, 1965).

Weber, Max, *Protestant Ethic and the Spirit of Capitalism*, trans. Talcott Parsons (New York: Scribners, 1958).

Weber, Max, Gunther Roth, and Claus Wittich, *Economy and Society: An Outline of Interpretive Sociology* (Berkeley: University of California Press, 1978).

Wentworth, Kara, *Performing the Slaughterhouse: Making Knowledge and Difference in Daily Practice*. Dissertation, University of California, San Diego, 2016.

Williams, Raymond, *Sociology of Culture* (Chicago: University of Chicago Press, 1981).

Williams, Rosalind, *Dream Worlds: Mass Consumption in Late Nineteenth-Century France* (Berkeley and Los Angeles: University of California Press, 1982).

Willis, Paul, *Learning to Labor: How Working Class Kids Get Working Class Jobs* (New York: Columbia University Press, 1981).

Wollstonecraft, Mary, *A Vindication of the Rights of Women* (London, 1792; Mineola, NY: Dover Publications, 1946).

Zelizer, Viviana, *Pricing the Priceless Child: The Changing Social Value of Children* (Princeton: Princeton University Press, 1994).

Zubrzycki, Geneviève, *The Crosses of Auschwitz* (Chicago: University of Chicago Press, 2006).

ACKNOWLEDGMENTS
FOR FIGURES

1.1   Photo Agency/Gemäldegalerie, Staatliche Museen zu Berlin/Jörg P. Anders

1.2   Wikimedia Commons

1.3   Web Gallery of Art/Wikimedia Commons

1.4   Marco Zanoli (sidonius 12:09, 2 May 2008 (UTC))

1.5   pwGhp-hQAnSBdg at Google Cultural Institute

1.6   Web Gallery of Art/Wikimedia Commons

1.7   The Yorck Project: 10.000 Meisterwerke der Malerei. DVD-ROM, 2002. ISBN 3936122202. Distributed by DIRECTMEDIA Publishing GmbH.

1.8   QAEccCsLDtbB4A at Google Cultural Institute

1.9   Web Gallery of Art/Wikimedia Commons

1.10 Web Gallery of Art/Wikimedia Commons

1.11 Wikimedia Commons

1.12 Web Gallery of Art/Wikimedia Commons

1.13 Wikimedia Commons

1.14 AFlvdukKgo bg at Google Cultural Institute

1.15 The Yorck Project: 10.000 Meisterwerke der Malerei. DVD-ROM, 2002. ISBN 3936122202. Distributed by DIRECTMEDIA Publishing GmbH

1.16 ZgHt6DZhk-6SVw at Google Cultural Institute

1.17 Louis XIV Collection/Wikimedia Commons

1.18 Les collections du château de Versailles/Wikimedia Commons

1.19 Photographie de Benoit Chain/Musée du Domaine départemental de Sceaux, reproduction sur autorisation NUM 2003_7_14.jpg

2.1   Wikimedia Commons

2.2   Wikimedia Commons

2.3   Web Gallery of Art/Wikimedia Commons

2.4   Wikimedia Commons

8.6 Wi1234/Wikimedia Commons

8.7 Antique Collector's Club

8.8 Bibliothèque nationale de France/Wikimedia Commons

8.9 still from "Monument Valley" Ustwo

9.1 Wikimedia Commons

9.2 Coen 2007. *No Country for Old Men*

9.3 Bildnachweis: ETH-Bibliothek Zürich, Bildarchiv/Fotograf: Unbekannt/Portr_03106

9.4 Williams 2010. *Where the Heart Is*

9.5 Williams 2010. *Where the Heart Is*

9.6 Williams 2010. *Where the Heart Is*

9.7 Dschwen/Wikimedia Commons

9.8 Emmerich 1996. *Independence Day*

10.1 Victoria and Albert Museum, London/Wikimedia Commons

10.2 Gillian Naylor, William Morris by Himself: Designs and Writings/Wikimedia Commons

10.3 Wikimedia Commons

10.4 ptwo/flickr

10.5 Getty

10.6 Pretzelpaws/Wikimedia Commons

10.7 Mona/Wikimedia Commons

10.8 Walter, Bernhard, Allgemeiner Deutscher Nachrichtendienst – Zentralbild (Bild 183)/Wikimedia Commons

10.9 Isreal Government Press Office/flickr

INDEX

Note: Page numbers in **bold** type refer to **figures**
Page numbers in *italic* type refer to *tables*